Crafting Novel AI:
Harnessing the Power of NLP for Writing

by Dr. Edward Franklin

Copyright ©2023 Dr. Edward Franklin. All Rights Reserved.

ISBN: 9781312286313

Imprint: Lulu.com

"Crafting Novel AI: Harnessing the Power of NLP for Writing" is a comprehensive guide that takes readers through the process of developing a natural language processing (NLP) AI tool for novel writing.

It begins with defining the scope, identifying goals, and researching existing tools.

User needs are analyzed, leading to the definition of key features that prioritize user experience and technical feasibility.

Functional and technical constraints are considered, and a requirements document is created.

Stakeholder input is sought and incorporated to refine the scope. As the project progresses, the scope is updated and refined based on new insights.

Thorough testing and iteration ensure the tool's effectiveness and usability.

Deployment factors are considered, and intellectual property protection is addressed. With expertise in machine learning, NLP, and software development, this guide empowers readers to create a customized NLP AI tool for novel writing.

Contents

1. Define the Scope — 11

Identify Goals and Objectives 13
Research Existing Tools 16
Analyze User Needs 19
Define Key Features 21
Prioritize Features 23
Set Functional and Technical Constraints 25
Create a Requirements Document 27
Seek Stakeholder Input 30
Update and Refine Scope 32

2. Data Collection — 37

Determine Dataset Requirements 39
Identify Data Sources 41
Obtain Permissions and Legal Considerations 43
Crawl or Download Data 45
Filter and Curate Data 47
Consider Data Augmentation (Optional) 49
Split Dataset 51
Ensure Data Privacy and Anonymity 53
Data Quality Control 55
Documentation and Metadata 57

3. Preprocessing　　　　　　　　　　61

Text Cleaning...63
Tokenization 66
Stopword Removal...68
Lowercasing 70
Lemmatization or Stemming...72
Removing Punctuation..75
Handling Special Cases 77
Normalization..80
Text Formatting...82

4. Training a Language Model　　　　85

Selecting a Base Model..87
Data Preparation 89
Tokenization 91
Encoding and Embedding 94
Model Architecture..97
Training Process..100
Hyperparameter Tuning 103
Validation and Evaluation...106
Saving the Trained Model...109

5. Fine Tuning　　　　　　　　　　　113

Selecting a Pre-trained Language Model.....................115
Dataset Preparation 117
Model Initialization 119
Training Objective 122
Fine-tuning Process...125
Hyperparameter Optimization 128
Validation and Evaluation...131
Iteration and Refinement 134

6. Implementing Novel Writing Features — 139

Introduction to Machine Learning Algorithms...................141
Grammar Checking..144
Style Suggestions...146
Character Development...148
Plot Analysis..150
Suggestion System..152
Real-time Feedback...154
Integration of Features...156
User Customization...158
Iterative Development..160

7. User Interface — 165

Define User Requirements..167
User Flow Design...169
Wireframing..171
Visual Design...173
Text Input/Output..175
Real-time Suggestions..178
User Preferences Customization.................................181
Usability Testing..185
Iteration and Enhancement......................................189

8. Testing and Iteration — 195

Test Scenario Design..197
Test Execution..200
Gather User Feedback..203
Analyze Feedback and Identify Issues...........................206
Iterative Development..207
Testing Enhancements..210
Continuous User Feedback.......................................212
Usability Testing..215
Performance Optimization.......................................218
Documentation and User Guides................................221

9. Deployment   225

Scalability Assessment 227
Infrastructure Setup 230
System Architecture Design 232
Implementation 234
Efficiency Optimization 237
Security Considerations 239
User Acceptance Testing 241
Documentation and Training 243
Deployment Strategy 245
Continuous Monitoring and Maintenance 247

10. Intellectual Property Protection   251

Consult with Legal Experts 253
Patent Protection 256
Copyright Protection 259
Trade Secret Protection 262
Non-Disclosure Agreements 265
Trademark Protection 268
Documentation and Record-Keeping 271
Monitoring and Enforcement 274
International Considerations 277
Ongoing Review and Maintenance 280

11. Collaboration and Expertise — 285

- Identify Skill Gaps 287
- Build a Team 290
- Define Roles and Responsibilities..293
- Collaborate on Design and Development.............................296
- Knowledge Sharing and Learning..299
- Continuous Communication 302
- Quality Assurance...305
- Documentation and Knowledge Management 308
- Project Management..311
- Continuous Learning and Improvement..............................314

1.

Define the Scope

Clearly define the specific features and functionalities you want your NLP AI to have for assisting in novel writing. Consider aspects such as grammar checking, style suggestions, character development, plot analysis, or any other specific requirements you envision.

Defining the scope of your natural language processing (NLP) AI tool for novel writing is a crucial initial step. It involves clearly outlining the specific features and functionalities you want your tool to have. Here are the detailed steps involved in defining the scope:

Identify Goals and Objectives

Determine the primary goals and objectives of your NLP AI tool. Consider what problem you aim to solve and how your tool can assist writers in novel writing. This could include improving grammar and style, enhancing character development, providing plot analysis, or any other specific requirements you envision.

Determine the Problem Statement

Clearly define the problem you aim to solve with your NLP AI tool for novel writing.

Identify the challenges and pain points faced by novel writers that you want to address.

For example, the problem could be to improve the quality of writing, enhance the efficiency of the writing process, or assist with specific aspects like grammar, style, character development, or plot analysis.

Establish the Overall Goals

Set the overarching goals for your NLP AI tool. These goals reflect the desired outcomes and impact you want to achieve.

Examples of goals could include improving the writing skills of novelists, enabling faster and more accurate editing, enhancing creativity in storytelling, or providing comprehensive writing assistance.

Define Specific Objectives

Break down the overall goals into specific objectives that are measurable and actionable.

Objectives should be focused on the features and functionalities of your NLP AI tool and their direct impact on addressing the identified problem.

For instance, specific objectives could be to develop a grammar checking algorithm, create a style suggestion module, implement a character development assistance feature, or provide plot analysis capabilities.

Consider User Needs and Expectations

Understand the needs, preferences, and expectations of your target users, which in this case are novel writers.

Conduct surveys, interviews, or user research to gather insights into their pain points, challenges, and desires related to novel writing.

Identify the specific requirements that novel writers have in terms of improving their writing skills, enhancing creativity, or streamlining the writing process.

Align Objectives with User Needs

Based on the gathered user insights, align the objectives of your NLP AI tool with the identified user needs and expectations.

Ensure that the objectives directly address the pain points and challenges faced by novel writers and offer valuable solutions.

Consider Innovations and Uniqueness

Evaluate potential innovations or unique features that could differentiate your NLP AI tool from existing solutions.

Identify areas where you can add value and improve upon the capabilities offered by other tools in the market.

Consider how your tool can provide novel and innovative approaches to address the needs of novel writers.

Define the Scope

Summarize the identified goals and objectives into a clear and concise scope statement.

This scope statement should serve as a guiding document throughout the development process.

It provides a shared understanding of the intended focus and direction of your NLP AI tool for novel writing.

DEFINE THE SCOPE

Defining the goals and objectives of your NLP AI tool sets the foundation for the entire development process. It ensures that you have a clear vision and direction, aligned with the needs of novel writers. The goals and objectives help guide subsequent steps, such as research, design, development, and testing, by providing a framework for building a tool that effectively addresses the specific needs of its users.

Research Existing Tools

Conduct research on existing NLP tools and solutions in the market. Explore the features and functionalities offered by these tools to gain insights and inspiration for your own tool. Identify gaps or areas for improvement that your tool can address.

Conduct Market Research

Begin by conducting comprehensive market research to identify existing NLP tools and solutions for novel writing.

Explore both commercial and open-source tools that are currently available in the market.

Consider tools specifically designed for writing assistance, grammar checking, style suggestions, character development, plot analysis, and any other relevant areas.

Explore Features and Functionalities

Dive into the features and functionalities offered by the identified tools.

Analyze how these tools assist writers in improving their writing skills and overcoming challenges in novel writing.

Make note of the strengths and weaknesses of each tool, and assess their suitability for meeting your defined goals and objectives.

Identify Gaps and Areas for Improvement

Evaluate the existing tools to identify gaps or areas where they fall short in addressing the needs of novel writers.

Look for functionalities that are missing or not adequately supported by the existing tools.

Identify opportunities to create a tool that offers unique features or provides enhanced performance in specific areas.

Consider User Feedback and Reviews

Examine user feedback, reviews, and testimonials related to the existing tools.

Analyze the common complaints, suggestions, and expectations expressed by writers who have used these tools.

Pay attention to the aspects that users appreciate and the areas where they feel the existing tools are lacking.

Understand Pricing and Licensing

Investigate the pricing models and licensing options associated with the existing tools.

Consider the affordability, scalability, and long-term costs associated with adopting these tools.

Evaluate whether there are opportunities to offer a more cost-effective solution or explore alternative pricing models.

Identify Innovations and Competitive Advantage

Look for innovative features or approaches offered by the existing tools that can inspire your own tool's development.

Determine how your NLP AI tool can differentiate itself and provide a competitive advantage in the market.

Focus on areas where you can offer unique functionalities or deliver an improved user experience.

Document Findings and Insights

Compile your research findings into a comprehensive document that outlines the strengths, weaknesses, and gaps of existing tools.

Include insights gained from user feedback, reviews, and pricing considerations.

Use this document as a reference throughout the development process to inform your decision-making and ensure your tool offers added value.

By conducting thorough research on existing NLP tools and solutions, you gain valuable insights and inspiration for your own NLP AI tool for novel writing. This research helps you identify areas for improvement, understand user expectations, and define unique features that set your tool apart. The findings from this research serve as a foundation for designing a tool that effectively meets the needs of novel writers and offers a competitive advantage in the market.

Analyze User Needs

Understand the needs and preferences of your target users, which in this case are novel writers. Conduct surveys, interviews, or user research to gather insights into their pain points, challenges, and expectations. This information will help you tailor your tool to meet their specific requirements.

Understanding the needs and preferences of your target users, novel writers, is a critical step in defining the scope of your natural language processing (NLP) AI tool. By conducting surveys, interviews, or user research, you can gather valuable insights into their pain points, challenges, and expectations. Here are the detailed steps involved in analyzing user needs:

Determine Research Methods

Choose the appropriate research methods to gather insights from novel writers. Surveys can be conducted online, allowing you to reach a large number of participants and collect quantitative data. Interviews provide an opportunity for in-depth discussions and qualitative insights. User research can involve observing writers in their writing process or analyzing their existing works.

Identify Participant Profiles

Define the characteristics of the novel writers you want to target. Consider their experience level, writing styles, genres they specialize in, and any other relevant factors that may influence their needs and preferences. This will help ensure that your research is focused and tailored to the specific user group.

Create Research Questions

Develop a set of research questions that will guide your investigation into user needs. These questions should cover various aspects related to novel writing, such as the challenges writers face, their expectations from an AI tool, the specific areas where they seek assistance, and any pain points they encounter in the writing process.

Conduct Surveys, Interviews, or User Research

Administer surveys, conduct interviews, or engage in user research activities to gather data directly from novel writers. Surveys can be distributed online, while interviews and user research can involve one-on-one interactions or observations. Use these methods to collect information that addresses your research questions and provides insights into the target users' needs.

Analyze Data

Thoroughly analyze the collected data to identify patterns, trends, and common themes. Use qualitative data analysis techniques, such as coding and categorization, to extract meaningful insights from open-ended responses. Quantitative data can be analyzed using statistical methods to derive key findings. Look for recurring patterns, pain points, and opportunities for improvement that emerge from the data.

Extract User Requirements

Based on the analyzed data, extract user requirements that reflect the needs and preferences of novel writers. These requirements should inform the features and functionalities you aim to incorporate into your NLP AI tool. Consider aspects such as the specific writing challenges writers face, the type of assistance they seek, their expectations regarding grammar and style, character development, plot analysis, and any other relevant areas.

Document User Insights

Document the findings from your user research in a comprehensive manner. This documentation should capture the pain points, challenges, expectations, and preferences expressed by novel writers. Use quotes, anecdotes, and data visualizations to present the insights in a compelling and accessible format.

By conducting thorough user needs analysis, you can gain a deep understanding of the requirements and expectations of novel writers. This knowledge will guide the development of your NLP AI tool, ensuring that it effectively addresses their specific needs and enhances their writing process.

Define Key Features

Based on your research and user needs analysis, define the key features and functionalities you want your NLP AI tool to have. Consider aspects such as grammar checking, style suggestions, character development assistance, plot analysis, or any other features that align with your objectives and user requirements.

After conducting research and analyzing the needs of novel writers, the next step in defining the scope of your natural language processing (NLP) AI tool is to identify the key features and functionalities you want your tool to have. This step involves carefully considering the aspects of novel writing that you aim to address and aligning them with the objectives and user requirements. Here are the detailed steps involved in defining the key features:

Review Research Findings

Revisit the insights gained from your research and user needs analysis. Consider the pain points, challenges, and expectations expressed by novel writers. Use these findings as a foundation for determining the key features your NLP AI tool should possess.

Identify Relevant Areas

Identify the specific areas in novel writing that your tool can address and improve upon. These areas may include grammar checking, style suggestions, character development assistance, plot analysis, dialogue optimization, pacing suggestions, or any other aspects that emerged as important to the target users.

Brainstorm Feature Ideas

Conduct brainstorming sessions to generate ideas for features and functionalities that align with the identified areas of improvement. Encourage creativity and explore innovative ways your NLP AI tool can assist writers in enhancing their novels. Consider both practical and imaginative features that could provide valuable support.

Evaluate Feasibility and Impact

Assess the feasibility and potential impact of each feature idea. Consider technical complexity, computational requirements, available resources, and time constraints. Evaluate how each feature would contribute to the overall user experience and how it aligns with the defined goals and objectives.

Prioritize Key Features

Prioritize the identified features based on their importance and feasibility. Consider the potential value they bring to the target users and the overall effectiveness of your NLP AI tool. Balance the desire to include all possible features with the need to deliver a high-quality product within the available resources.

Create Feature Descriptions

For each key feature, create detailed descriptions that outline its functionality and purpose. Clearly articulate how each feature addresses the identified pain points and enhances the novel writing process. Use these descriptions as a reference for development and communication with the development team.

Align Features with User Requirements

Ensure that the key features align with the user requirements derived from the research and user needs analysis. Verify that each feature directly addresses the identified needs and preferences of novel writers and contributes to solving their problems or enhancing their writing experience.

Defining the key features of your NLP AI tool is essential for guiding the subsequent steps of development. It provides a clear roadmap for data collection, preprocessing, model training, and the implementation of novel writing functionalities. By focusing on the identified key features, you can ensure that your tool effectively meets the specific needs of novel writers and delivers a valuable and impactful solution.

Prioritize Features

Once you have identified the key features, prioritize them based on their importance and feasibility. Consider the impact of each feature on the overall user experience and the technical complexity involved in implementing them.

Once you have identified the key features for your natural language processing (NLP) AI tool for novel writing, the next step is to prioritize them based on their importance and feasibility. This process involves considering the impact of each feature on the overall user experience and assessing the technical complexity involved in implementing them. Here are the detailed steps involved in prioritizing features:

Evaluate Importance

Assess the significance and value of each key feature in addressing the goals and objectives of your NLP AI tool. Consider how each feature contributes to solving the identified problems or enhancing the writing process for novel writers. Prioritize features that have a higher impact on improving the overall user experience and achieving the desired outcomes.

Consider Feasibility

Evaluate the technical complexity of implementing each feature. Take into account factors such as available resources, expertise, time constraints, and computational requirements. Consider whether the development of a particular feature is feasible within the given constraints and resources.

Assess Dependencies

Analyze the interdependencies among the features. Determine if certain features rely on the successful implementation of other features. Consider the dependencies when establishing the order of feature prioritization, ensuring that foundational features are addressed first.

Seek User Input

Gather feedback from the target users, such as novel writers, to understand their preferences and priorities. Conduct surveys, interviews, or user research to obtain insights on which features are most important to them. Incorporate user input into the prioritization process to align the tool with the needs and expectations of the users.

Weight Importance and Feasibility

Assign weights or scores to each feature based on their importance and feasibility. This helps quantify the relative priority of each feature and provides a basis for decision-making during the development process. Consider using a scoring system or other prioritization techniques to objectively assess and compare features.

Collaborate with Stakeholders

Collaborate with stakeholders, including writers, editors, or industry experts, to validate the prioritization of features. Seek their input and insights on the importance and feasibility of the identified features. Incorporate their feedback into the prioritization process to ensure that the tool meets the requirements and expectations of all stakeholders.

Finalize Feature Prioritization

Based on the evaluation of importance, feasibility, user input, and stakeholder collaboration, finalize the prioritization of features. Create a prioritized list or roadmap that outlines the order in which the features will be implemented. Ensure that the most critical and achievable features are given higher priority.

By prioritizing features, you ensure that the development efforts are focused on delivering the most valuable and impactful functionalities for your NLP AI tool. This approach helps allocate resources efficiently, manage expectations, and guide the subsequent steps of data collection, preprocessing, model training, and implementation of the prioritized features.

Set Functional and Technical Constraints

Determine any functional or technical constraints that may impact the development of your tool. These constraints could include limitations in computational resources, available data, or specific requirements from stakeholders or users.

Determining functional and technical constraints is an important step in defining the scope of your natural language processing (NLP) AI tool for novel writing. These constraints help identify the limitations and considerations that may impact the development of your tool. Here are the detailed steps involved in setting functional and technical constraints:

Assess Computational Resources

Evaluate the available computational resources, such as hardware capabilities and processing power, that will be utilized for developing and running your NLP AI tool. Consider factors like CPU, GPU, memory, and storage capacity. Determine the limitations and capabilities of the resources to ensure that your tool can be effectively implemented within the available infrastructure.

Consider Data Availability

Evaluate the availability and accessibility of data required for training and testing your NLP model. Assess whether you have sufficient novel texts or other relevant datasets to train the AI model effectively. Consider any limitations in terms of the quantity, quality, or diversity of available data that may impact the performance or generalization capabilities of your tool.

Identify Technical Requirements

Identify any specific technical requirements that need to be met for the successful development and deployment of your NLP AI tool. These requirements may include compatibility with specific programming languages, frameworks, or libraries, as well as adherence to industry standards or protocols. Consider any dependencies or constraints related to software or hardware technologies that may affect the implementation process.

Account for Available APIs and Tools

Explore existing APIs and tools that you can leverage to enhance the functionality of your NLP AI tool. Determine if there are any limitations or restrictions imposed by these APIs or tools in terms of usage, access, or integration. Consider whether you need to obtain licenses, comply with usage policies, or account for potential changes or limitations in the future.

Identify Stakeholder Requirements

Collaborate with stakeholders, such as writers, editors, or industry experts, to identify any specific functional or technical requirements they may have. Take into account their preferences, expectations, and specific needs when defining the constraints. Incorporate their input and insights to ensure that the tool aligns with their requirements.

Document the Constraints

Document the identified functional and technical constraints in your requirements document. Clearly specify the limitations, considerations, and requirements related to computational resources, data availability, technical dependencies, and stakeholder needs. This documentation serves as a reference for the development team, guiding them in building the tool within the defined constraints.

Setting functional and technical constraints helps you make informed decisions and address potential challenges during the development process of your NLP AI tool. By considering these constraints, you ensure that your tool can be effectively implemented, meets the necessary technical requirements, and aligns with the available resources and stakeholder expectations.

Create a Requirements Document

Document the defined scope, goals, objectives, and prioritized features in a requirements document. This document serves as a reference throughout the development process, ensuring that the development team stays aligned with the project's objectives.

Creating a requirements document is an important step in defining the scope of your natural language processing (NLP) AI tool for novel writing. This document serves as a reference throughout the development process, ensuring that the development team stays aligned with the project's objectives. Here are the detailed steps involved in creating a requirements document:

Define Document Structure

Determine the structure and format of the requirements document. Consider including sections such as an introduction, project objectives, scope, key features, functional requirements, technical requirements, and any other relevant sections that provide a comprehensive overview of the project.

Introduction

Begin the requirements document with an introduction that provides an overview of the project, its goals, and its intended audience. This section should clearly explain the purpose of the document and set the context for the following sections.

Project Objectives

Clearly state the primary goals and objectives of your NLP AI tool. Refer to the information gathered in step 1.1 to identify the specific problem you aim to solve and how your tool will assist writers in novel writing. This section should outline the overall purpose of the tool.

Scope

Document the defined scope of your NLP AI tool. This includes the specific features and functionalities that you want your tool to have, as determined in step 1.4. Clearly describe the scope of each feature and its intended impact on the user experience.

Key Features

Provide a detailed description of each key feature identified in step 1.4. Explain the functionality, purpose, and expected outcomes of each feature. Consider including examples or use cases to illustrate how each feature will benefit the users.

Functional Requirements

Document the functional requirements of your NLP AI tool. Specify how each feature should behave and outline any specific user interactions or system behaviors that need to be implemented. Be clear and precise in defining the desired functionality.

Technical Requirements

Specify the technical requirements that need to be considered during the development of your tool. This can include hardware specifications, software dependencies, performance expectations, scalability requirements, data storage and processing requirements, and any other technical considerations necessary for the successful implementation of your tool.

Collaboration and Validation

Explain the collaborative approach taken in seeking stakeholder input, as described in step 1.8. Document the feedback and insights gathered from stakeholders, such as writers, editors, or industry experts, and describe how they have influenced the scope and requirements of your tool.

Maintenance and Update

Describe how the requirements document will be maintained and updated throughout the development process. Clarify the process for incorporating changes, additions, or refinements to the scope and requirements as the project progresses, as described in step 1.9.

Review and Approval

Set up a review and approval process for the requirements document. This may involve sharing the document with relevant stakeholders and obtaining their feedback and approval. Ensure that all stakeholders are aligned with the document and address any concerns or suggestions they may have.

By creating a comprehensive requirements document, you establish a clear vision and direction for the development of your NLP AI tool. This document serves as a reference point for the development team, guiding subsequent steps such as data collection, preprocessing, and model training. It helps ensure that the tool is built to meet the specific needs of novel writers and stays aligned with the defined objectives.

Seek Stakeholder Input

Collaborate with stakeholders, such as writers, editors, or industry experts, to gather their input and validate the defined scope. Incorporate their feedback and insights to refine and enhance the scope of your tool.

Collaborating with stakeholders is an important step in defining the scope of your natural language processing (NLP) AI tool for novel writing. By gathering input from writers, editors, industry experts, and other relevant stakeholders, you can validate and enhance the defined scope. Here are the detailed steps involved in seeking stakeholder input:

Identify Relevant Stakeholders

Determine the key stakeholders who can provide valuable insights and feedback on your NLP AI tool. This may include novel writers, experienced editors, literary agents, publishers, or industry experts. Consider their expertise and involvement in the novel writing process.

Schedule Meetings or Workshops

Arrange meetings, workshops, or focus groups to engage with the stakeholders. These sessions can be conducted in person or remotely, depending on the availability and preferences of the stakeholders. Ensure that the necessary communication channels are established for effective collaboration.

Share Project Overview

Present an overview of your NLP AI tool project to the stakeholders. Explain the purpose, goals, and potential benefits of the tool. Provide a clear understanding of how the tool aims to assist writers in novel writing and the specific features and functionalities it offers.

Gather Feedback and Insights

Encourage stakeholders to share their perspectives, opinions, and suggestions regarding the defined scope and key features of the tool. Ask open-ended questions to stimulate discussions and gather comprehensive feedback. Consider their pain points, challenges, expectations, and ideas for improvement.

Incorporate Stakeholder Insights

Carefully analyze and evaluate the feedback received from stakeholders. Identify common themes, patterns, or areas for improvement that align with the project's goals and objectives. Incorporate the valuable insights into refining and enhancing the scope of your NLP AI tool.

Address Concerns and Questions

Address any concerns, questions, or misconceptions raised by the stakeholders. Ensure that their feedback is acknowledged and responded to appropriately. Provide clarifications or additional information to resolve any uncertainties and foster a collaborative environment.

Document Stakeholder Feedback

Document the feedback and insights received from the stakeholders. This documentation serves as a reference for future decision-making and ensures that the stakeholders' perspectives are properly considered during the development process. Update the requirements document (as mentioned in step 1.7) to reflect the refined scope based on stakeholder input.

Follow-Up and Communication

Maintain open lines of communication with the stakeholders throughout the development process. Provide regular updates on the progress of the project and how their input has influenced the tool's scope and development. Seek additional feedback or clarification when needed.

By seeking stakeholder input, you gain valuable perspectives and expertise that can help shape your NLP AI tool to better meet the needs of novel writers. The collaboration with stakeholders ensures that the tool aligns with industry expectations, enhances the writing process, and addresses specific pain points or challenges faced by writers.

Update and Refine Scope

As the project progresses and you gain more insights, be open to revisiting and refining the scope. Adjust the features and functionalities based on new discoveries or changing requirements to ensure that your NLP AI tool aligns with the evolving needs of your target users.

As your NLP AI tool project progresses and you gather more insights, it is important to be open to revisiting and refining the scope to ensure that it aligns with the evolving needs of your target users. This step allows you to adjust the features and functionalities based on new discoveries or changing requirements. Here are the detailed steps involved in updating and refining the scope:

Review User Feedback

Evaluate the feedback received from users, stakeholders, and other relevant parties throughout the development process. Analyze their input, comments, and suggestions regarding the existing features and functionalities of your NLP AI tool. Identify patterns, common themes, and areas for improvement.

Identify New Discoveries

Pay attention to any new insights, trends, or requirements that emerge during the development or testing phase of your tool. These discoveries could come from user feedback, industry advancements, or technological advancements. Assess how these new findings can enhance or modify the scope of your NLP AI tool.

Conduct Market Analysis

Continuously monitor the market for novel writing tools, NLP advancements, and emerging technologies. Stay updated on industry trends, competitor offerings, and user demands. Evaluate how these market dynamics may impact your tool's scope and consider incorporating relevant features or improvements.

Evaluate Technical Feasibility

Consider the technical feasibility of implementing new features or functionalities within your NLP AI tool. Assess the computational resources, data requirements, and infrastructure needed to support the changes. Determine if any technical constraints exist that could impact the feasibility of incorporating new elements.

Assess Impact on User Experience

Analyze the impact of potential scope updates on the overall user experience. Consider how the proposed changes may affect the tool's usability, performance, and effectiveness in assisting novel writers. Strive to maintain a balance between introducing new features and ensuring a smooth and intuitive user interface.

Engage with Stakeholders

Collaborate with stakeholders, such as writers, editors, industry experts, or development team members, to discuss potential scope updates. Seek their input and insights on the proposed changes, and gather their perspectives on how these updates align with the project's objectives and user requirements.

Document Scope Revisions

Update the requirements document (mentioned in step 1.7) to reflect the refined scope of your NLP AI tool. Clearly document the modifications, additions, or removals of features and functionalities. Ensure that the document accurately represents the updated vision and direction of the tool.

Communicate Scope Changes

Share the revised scope with the relevant stakeholders and team members. Communicate the reasons behind the updates, highlighting the insights, feedback, or new discoveries that led to the changes. Ensure that everyone involved in the project understands and agrees upon the refined scope.

Iterate and Repeat

Recognize that refining the scope is an iterative process. As you progress through subsequent development stages, continuously evaluate the effectiveness and impact of the scope updates. Gather further feedback, conduct testing, and refine the tool based on user interactions and market dynamics.

By updating and refining the scope of your NLP AI tool, you ensure that it remains aligned with the evolving needs of novel writers and takes advantage of new discoveries and insights. This iterative approach allows you to adapt your tool to the changing landscape and deliver a solution that effectively assists writers in their novel writing endeavors.

Defining the scope of your NLP AI tool is crucial to ensure that you have a clear vision and direction for development. It helps guide subsequent steps, such as data collection, preprocessing, and model training, by providing a framework for building the tool that meets the specific needs of novel writers.

DEFINE THE SCOPE

2.

Data Collection

Gather a large dataset of novel texts that will serve as training data for your NLP model. This dataset should cover a wide range of genres, writing styles, and themes to ensure the AI's generalization capabilities.

Data collection is a crucial step in creating your own natural language processing (NLP) AI for novel writing. It involves gathering a large dataset of novel texts that will serve as the training data for your NLP model. Here are the detailed steps involved in the data collection process:

Determine Dataset Requirements

In order to create a powerful natural language processing (NLP) model for crafting novel AI, you need to start by collecting the right dataset that aligns with your project goals. The dataset should be diverse, representative, and substantial enough to provide meaningful insights and patterns. Here's a step-by-step guide to help you determine the dataset requirements for your NLP project:

Step 1: Define Project Goals and Objectives

Clearly define the goals and objectives of your NLP project. Decide what specific tasks you want your AI model to accomplish, such as grammar checking, style suggestions, character development, plot analysis, and more. This will guide you in identifying the type of text data you need to collect.

Step 2: Identify Target Text Domain

Based on your project goals, identify the domain of texts you want your AI model to work with. For example, if you aim to create a novel-writing AI, you might want to collect a dataset of fiction books, novels, short stories, or other creative writing.

Step 3: Determine Data Size

Estimate the size of the dataset you'll need. The dataset should be large enough to cover a wide range of writing styles and themes while providing sufficient examples for the AI model to learn effectively. The actual size will depend on the complexity of your project and the resources available for training.

Step 4: Data Annotation Requirements

Decide if your dataset requires any manual annotation. For example, if you want to include character attributes for character development, you'll need annotated data that labels each character's traits, relationships, etc.

Step 5: Open Source vs. Proprietary Data

Consider whether you'll use existing open-source datasets or need to collect proprietary data. Open-source datasets are readily available but may not always align perfectly with your project's objectives. Proprietary data, on the other hand, might require permissions and legal considerations.

Step 6: Data Balance and Bias

Pay attention to data balance and potential biases. Ensure that your dataset includes a fair representation of different writing styles, genres, and perspectives. Biased datasets could lead to biased AI outputs.

Step 7: Ethical Considerations

Take ethical considerations into account when collecting and using data. Protect user privacy, anonymize sensitive information, and avoid using data that may be harmful or discriminatory.

Step 8: Data Licensing and Copyright

Understand the licensing and copyright implications of the data you collect. Ensure that you have the right to use and distribute the data for your AI project.

Step 9: Data Source Documentation

Maintain detailed documentation of the data sources, including the origin of the data, licensing terms, and any pre-processing steps performed on the data.

Step 10: Explore Available Datasets

Search for existing datasets that align with your project goals. There are various sources for datasets, including Kaggle, academic repositories, government data portals, and specialized NLP datasets like the Common Crawl or the Gutenberg Project.

Step 11: Evaluate Data Quality

Carefully assess the quality of the datasets you consider using. Check for data errors, missing values, and inconsistencies that may impact the performance of your AI model.

Step 12: Data Collection Plan

Based on your dataset requirements, create a data collection plan outlining the specific steps you'll take to acquire, filter, and curate the data.

Remember that the quality and relevance of your dataset play a critical role in the success of your NLP model. Take your time during this phase, as a well-prepared dataset will lay a strong foundation for crafting your novel AI.

Identify Data Sources

Once you have determined the dataset requirements for your novel-writing AI project, the next step is to identify the data sources from which you will collect the necessary text data. In this section, we'll explore the process of finding relevant data sources and gathering the data needed for your NLP model. Here's a step-by-step guide:

Step 1: Identify Potential Data Sources

Begin by brainstorming and identifying potential data sources that align with your project goals. Some common data sources for text data include:

a) Online Text Corpora: Websites hosting a large collection of texts, such as Project Gutenberg, Common Crawl, Open Web Text Corpus, or Wikipedia.

b) Digital Libraries: Online repositories of books, articles, research papers, and other written content.

c) Social Media: Platforms like Twitter, Reddit, or blogs can provide valuable text data for training and testing your AI model.

d) Specific Websites: If your project focuses on a particular domain (e.g., movie reviews or news articles), consider scraping data from relevant websites.

e) APIs: Some platforms offer APIs that allow you to access and retrieve text data programmatically. For instance, Twitter's API allows you to access tweets.

f) Public Datasets: Look for publicly available datasets that suit your project objectives. Websites like Kaggle often host datasets related to various domains.

Step 2: Assess Data Quality and Relevance

Evaluate the potential data sources based on data quality and relevance to your project. Consider factors such as data accuracy, completeness, domain coverage, and the presence of any biases. It's crucial to ensure that the data collected is representative of the writing styles and themes you want your AI model to handle.

Step 3: Check Licensing and Copyright

Before proceeding, make sure to review the licensing terms and copyright restrictions associated with each data source. Ensure that you have the right to use the data for your AI project and comply with any usage limitations.

Step 4: Web Scraping (if applicable)

If you choose to collect data from websites or platforms that do not offer downloadable datasets, you may need to perform web scraping. Python provides libraries like Beautiful Soup and Scrapy that can help you extract text data from websites. However, remember to adhere to website terms of service and avoid overloading servers with excessive requests.

Step 5: Data Download and Storage

For datasets available for download, follow the instructions provided by the data source to obtain the data files. Download the data and store it in an organized manner on your local machine or server.

Step 6: Data Format and Conversion

Ensure that the data you collected is in a format suitable for processing. Common formats for text data include plain text files (.txt), CSV files, or JSON files. If necessary, convert the data to the appropriate format for further processing.

Step 7: Combine Multiple Sources (if applicable)

If you are using data from multiple sources, you may need to combine the datasets to create a unified dataset for training and testing your AI model. Python provides libraries like Pandas for data manipulation and merging.

Step 8: Data Sampling (Optional)

Depending on the size of your dataset and the resources available, you might consider taking a random sample of the data to work with during the initial stages of development. Sampling can be useful for rapid prototyping and experimentation.

Step 9: Data Backup and Version Control

Always create backups of your collected data and use version control tools like Git to track changes and manage different versions of the dataset.

By completing these steps, you'll have successfully identified and collected the necessary text data from relevant sources. This data will serve as the foundation for training and fine-tuning your novel-writing AI model. Remember to keep your data documentation updated, including information about the data sources, collection dates, and any modifications made during the data filtering and curation process.

Obtain Permissions and Legal Considerations

Before proceeding with data collection for your novel-writing AI project, it is crucial to ensure that you have the necessary permissions and adhere to legal considerations regarding the data you intend to use. This section will guide you through the process of obtaining permissions and handling legal aspects related to data collection. Here's a step-by-step guide:

Step 1: Determine Data Usage Rights

Identify the type of data you plan to collect and its usage rights. Some datasets may come with specific usage licenses, while others may be freely available for any purpose. It's essential to read and understand the terms and conditions associated with the data sources you intend to use.

Step 2: Check for Copyright Restrictions

Verify that the data you plan to collect does not violate any copyright laws or intellectual property rights. If the data is copyrighted, ensure that you have the necessary permissions to use it for your AI project.

Step 3: Seek Data Owner's Permission

If you are collecting data from individuals or organizations, reach out to the data owners and request explicit permission to use their data. This is especially important if you plan to use data that is not publicly available or is subject to privacy concerns.

Step 4: Handle Sensitive and Personal Information

If your dataset contains sensitive or personal information about individuals, ensure that you comply with data protection and privacy laws. Anonymize or pseudonymize the data when necessary to protect the privacy of individuals.

Step 5: Follow Web Scraping Guidelines

If you are using web scraping to collect data from websites, check the website's terms of service and robots.txt file for any scraping restrictions. Respect website guidelines and avoid aggressive scraping that could cause server overload or disrupt the website's operations.

Step 6: Keep Detailed Records

Maintain detailed records of the permissions obtained and the legal agreements made with data owners. This documentation is essential for demonstrating compliance with data usage rights and protecting yourself from potential legal issues.

Step 7: Consult Legal Experts (if necessary)

If you are uncertain about any legal aspects of data collection, it's wise to seek advice from legal experts familiar with data protection and intellectual property laws. They can provide guidance specific to your project's needs and help you navigate potential legal challenges.

Step 8: Terms of Use and Privacy Policy

If you plan to make your AI model available to users, develop a clear and comprehensive terms of use and privacy policy. Inform users about how their data will be used and stored, and obtain their consent for data collection and processing.

Step 9: Data License (if applicable)

If you are sharing your AI model or the collected dataset with others, consider licensing the data under appropriate open-source or proprietary licenses. Choose a license that aligns with your project's goals and encourages responsible data sharing.

Remember that data collection involves a great deal of responsibility, and legal compliance is crucial to avoid potential legal repercussions. Take the time to carefully handle permissions and legal considerations during the data collection phase, as it will set the groundwork for the rest of your novel-writing AI project.

Crawl or Download Data

In the process of data collection for your novel-writing AI project, you may need to gather textual data from various online sources, such as websites, digital libraries, or social media platforms. One way to obtain such data is through web crawling or downloading. This section will guide you through the steps of web crawling or downloading data for your NLP project. Here's a step-by-step guide:

Step 1: Identify Target Websites or Sources

Begin by identifying the websites or online sources from which you want to collect data. These sources should align with the domain and writing styles relevant to your novel-writing AI project. For example, you might consider collecting data from literary forums, fiction blogs, or online bookstores.

Step 2: Check Website Policies and Terms of Service

Before proceeding with web crawling, review the website's policies and terms of service. Some websites explicitly forbid web scraping, while others may have specific rules or guidelines for data extraction. Respect the website's policies and ensure that you are allowed to crawl or download the data.

Step 3: Choose a Web Scraping Tool

Select a web scraping tool that suits your project's needs. Popular web scraping libraries in Python include Beautiful Soup and Scrapy. These libraries help you extract data from websites by parsing the HTML structure.

Step 4: Set Up Your Environment

Install the chosen web scraping library and its dependencies in your Python environment. If you're using a virtual environment, activate it to isolate your project dependencies.

Step 5: Navigate to Web Pages and Extract Data

Use the web scraping library to navigate to the web pages that contain the text data you want to collect. Extract the relevant information, such as blog posts, book reviews, or other written content, from the HTML elements on the page.

Here's an example of using Beautiful Soup to extract text data from a webpage:

```python
import requests
```

```
from bs4 import BeautifulSoup

# Replace 'url_to_scrape' with the actual URL of the webpage
you want to scrape
url_to_scrape = 'https://example.com'
response = requests.get(url_to_scrape)
soup = BeautifulSoup(response.text, 'html.parser')

# Use Beautiful Soup to find the HTML elements containing
the text data you need
text_data = []
for element in soup.find_all('p'):  # Replace 'p' with the
appropriate HTML tag containing the text data
    text_data.append(element.get_text())

# Now, 'text_data' contains the extracted text from the
webpage
print(text_data)
```

Step 6: Handle Pagination and Crawling Rules (if applicable)If the data you need is spread across multiple pages or follows a specific pagination pattern, implement the logic to navigate through the pages and extract the data accordingly. Ensure that your web scraping process adheres to the website's crawling rules and does not overload the server.

Step 7: Data Storage and Organization

After collecting the text data, store it in an organized manner. You may choose to save the data in plain text files (.txt) or structured formats like CSV or JSON. Properly label and categorize the data to maintain its integrity.

Step 8: Respect Website Politeness and Legal Considerations

While web crawling, make sure to be polite and considerate towards the websites you're extracting data from. Avoid making too many requests in a short period, as this can strain the website's servers and lead to unintended consequences. Additionally, comply with any legal considerations and copyright restrictions associated with the data you collect.

By following these steps, you can crawl or download the necessary data for your novel-writing AI project, enabling you to create a diverse and rich dataset for training and fine-tuning your NLP model.

Filter and Curate Data

Once you have obtained the raw data for your novel-writing AI project, the next step is to filter and curate the data. This process involves selecting relevant samples, removing noise and irrelevant information, and ensuring the dataset is of high quality. Here's a step-by-step guide on how to filter and curate your data:

Step 1: Define Inclusion and Exclusion Criteria

Start by defining clear criteria for including or excluding data samples from your dataset. Consider factors such as data relevance, quality, and alignment with your project objectives. For example, if your AI model is intended to write science fiction stories, you might exclude data related to historical events.

Step 2: Data Cleaning

Before filtering, perform data cleaning to handle any inconsistencies, errors, or missing information in your dataset. This step may involve removing duplicates, correcting typos, and resolving other data quality issues.

Step 3: Remove Irrelevant Data

Based on the defined criteria, remove any data samples that do not meet the inclusion criteria or are deemed irrelevant for your AI model's training and fine-tuning. This step helps ensure that your dataset contains only data that is directly useful for your novel-writing project.

Step 4: Manage Class Imbalance (if applicable)

If your dataset contains multiple classes or categories (e.g., different writing styles or genres), check for class imbalance. Class imbalance occurs when some categories have significantly more or fewer samples than others. To address this, you can perform oversampling or undersampling techniques to balance the classes and avoid biases in your AI model.

Step 5: Handle Outliers (if applicable)

If your dataset contains outliers or extreme data points that do not represent typical writing patterns, consider handling them appropriately. Outliers can adversely affect your AI model's performance, so you may choose to remove them or apply data transformations.

Step 6: Verify Data Licensing and Copyright

Ensure that the data samples in your curated dataset adhere to the necessary licensing and copyright requirements. Confirm that you have the rights to use and distribute the data in accordance with your project's goals.

Step 7: Data Splitting

Once the data filtering and curation process is complete, split your dataset into three main subsets: training data, validation data, and testing data. The training set is used to train your AI model, the validation set helps tune hyperparameters and assess model performance during training, and the testing set evaluates the final performance of the trained model.

Step 8: Save the Curated Dataset

Save the curated dataset in an appropriate format for further processing and model training. Common formats include plain text files, CSV files, or JSON files. Properly label and organize the data for easy access during the training phase.

Data filtering and curation play a vital role in building a high-quality dataset, which, in turn, contributes to the success of your novel-writing AI model. Be thorough in defining the inclusion and exclusion criteria, as well as in ensuring that the curated dataset represents the writing styles and themes you want your AI model to learn and generate.

Consider Data Augmentation (Optional)

Data augmentation is a technique used to increase the size and diversity of your dataset by generating new samples from the existing data. This process helps improve the generalization and robustness of your novel-writing AI model by exposing it to a broader range of writing styles and variations. Data augmentation is particularly useful when the initial dataset is limited or imbalanced. While this step is optional, it can significantly enhance the performance of your language model. Here's a step-by-step guide on how to consider data augmentation for your NLP project:

Step 1: Identify Suitable Data Augmentation Techniques

First, identify the data augmentation techniques that are appropriate for your novel-writing AI project. Some common data augmentation techniques for NLP include:

Synonym Replacement: Replace certain words with their synonyms to introduce word variations.

Random Insertion: Randomly insert additional words into sentences to create new variations.

Random Deletion: Randomly remove words from sentences to simulate missing or incomplete text.

Random Swap: Randomly swap the positions of words in a sentence to create different sentence structures.

Back Translation: Translate sentences to another language and then back to the original language to generate new sentences with similar meaning.

Step 2: Implement Data Augmentation

Depending on the selected data augmentation techniques, you can use existing NLP libraries or create custom functions to implement data augmentation. Python libraries like NLTK (Natural Language Toolkit) and AugmentText can be helpful in this process.

Here's an example of using the AugmentText library for synonym replacement:

```python
from AugmentText import Augment

# Initialize the augmenter
```

```
augmenter = Augment()

# Replace synonyms in a sentence
original_sentence = "The quick brown fox jumps over the lazy
dog."
augmented_sentences = augmenter.synonym_
replacement(original_sentence, num_aug=5)

# Print the augmented sentences
for sentence in augmented_sentences:
    print(sentence)
```

Step 3: Set Data Augmentation Parameters

When applying data augmentation, you can control the degree and extent of augmentation by setting parameters such as the number of augmented samples per original sample (num_aug), the probability of applying each augmentation technique, and the level of word replacement or modification.

Step 4: Combine Augmented Data with the Original Dataset

After generating augmented samples, combine them with the original dataset. This combined dataset now contains a more diverse and larger set of samples, ready for further preprocessing and training.

Step 5: Data Splitting (Optional)

If you augmented the dataset before splitting it into training, validation, and testing sets (as described in Section 2.7), make sure to perform the data splitting on the augmented dataset.

Step 6: Verify Dataset Quality

Inspect the augmented dataset to ensure that the generated samples are of sufficient quality and do not introduce nonsensical or irrelevant text. Manual inspection or using automated quality control techniques can help identify any issues.

Data augmentation can significantly enrich your dataset and improve the performance of your novel-writing AI model. However, it is essential to strike a balance and avoid over-augmenting, which could lead to noisy or less meaningful data. Experiment with different augmentation techniques and parameters to find the best approach for your specific NLP project.

Split Dataset

Once you have collected and curated your dataset, the next step is to split it into separate subsets for training, validation, and testing. Splitting the dataset ensures that your novel-writing AI model is trained on one portion of the data, validated on another portion to tune hyperparameters, and finally tested on a separate portion to assess its performance. Here's a step-by-step guide on how to split your dataset:

Step 1: Determine the Split Ratios

Decide on the proportions of data you want to allocate for training, validation, and testing. Common split ratios are often 70-15-15 or 80-10-10, but you can adjust these ratios based on the size and characteristics of your dataset.

Step 2: Shuffle the Dataset

Before splitting the data, it's essential to shuffle the dataset randomly. Shuffling ensures that the data is mixed and not sorted based on any particular order. This prevents bias during training and testing.

Step 3: Split the Dataset

Use your preferred programming language and libraries to split the dataset into training, validation, and testing sets. For example, in Python, you can use the scikit-learn library for this purpose:

```python
import numpy as np
from sklearn.model_selection import train_test_split

# Assuming you have a list of sentences (texts) and
corresponding labels (targets)
sentences = [...]  # List of sentences
labels = [...]  # List of corresponding labels

# Split the dataset into training, validation, and testing
sets
train_sentences, temp_sentences, train_labels, temp_labels = train_test_split(sentences, labels, test_size=0.3, random_state=42)
val_sentences, test_sentences, val_labels, test_labels = train_test_split(temp_sentences, temp_labels, test_size=0.5, random_state=42)

# Ensure the sizes of the splits
print("Training set size:", len(train_sentences))
print("Validation set size:", len(val_sentences))
print("Testing set size:", len(test_sentences))
```

In this example, the dataset is split into 70% for training, 15% for validation, and 15% for testing.

Step 4: Data Formatting

Ensure that the data is formatted correctly for further processing. For NLP tasks, this often involves converting text data into numerical representations using techniques like tokenization and encoding.

Step 5: Data Preprocessing (Optional)

Depending on the specific NLP tasks and models, you might need to perform additional data preprocessing steps on each split separately. These steps may include tokenization, stopword removal, and other text cleaning techniques, as outlined in Section 3.

Step 6: Save the Split Datasets

Save the training, validation, and testing sets into separate files or data structures. This will make it easier to load and use them in subsequent steps of your novel-writing AI project.

By splitting your dataset, you create distinct subsets for training, validation, and testing, enabling you to train and evaluate your novel-writing AI model effectively. Additionally, it helps prevent overfitting and ensures the generalization of your model to new, unseen data.

Ensure Data Privacy and Anonymity

Data privacy and anonymity are critical considerations when collecting and handling data, especially when dealing with personal or sensitive information. Protecting user data not only ensures compliance with legal and ethical standards but also builds trust with stakeholders. Here's a step-by-step guide on how to ensure data privacy and anonymity during the data collection process:

Step 1: Understand Privacy Requirements

Identify the specific privacy requirements relevant to your project. Depending on the nature of your data and the jurisdiction in which you operate, you may need to comply with data protection laws, such as the General Data Protection Regulation (GDPR) in the European Union or the California Consumer Privacy Act (CCPA) in the United States. Familiarize yourself with the regulations and obligations that apply to your project.

Step 2: Anonymization Techniques

Consider using anonymization techniques to remove or obfuscate any personally identifiable information (PII) from the collected data. PII includes names, addresses, phone numbers, email addresses, and any other information that could be used to identify an individual. Anonymization helps protect the privacy of individuals in the dataset.

Step 3: Aggregation and Generalization

Aggregate and generalize data when possible to further protect privacy. For example, instead of recording individual ages, group them into age ranges (e.g., 20-30, 31-40) to prevent identification of specific individuals. Similarly, aggregate location data to broader regions rather than exact addresses.

Step 4: Secure Data Storage

Ensure that the collected data is stored securely. Implement strong access controls, encryption, and other security measures to safeguard the data from unauthorized access or breaches.

Step 5: Data Sharing and Access Control

If you plan to share the dataset with collaborators or stakeholders, establish clear data sharing agreements and access controls. Limit access to only those individuals who need it for the specific purposes defined in the project scope.

Step 6: Informed Consent

Obtain informed consent from data subjects when necessary. Informed consent means that individuals are fully aware of how their data will be used and have given explicit permission for its use.

Step 7: Legal Review

Consider seeking legal advice or review to ensure that your data collection practices align with relevant privacy laws and regulations. Legal experts can help you identify potential risks and ensure compliance.

Step 8: Data Retention Policy

Define a data retention policy that specifies how long the collected data will be stored and when it should be securely deleted or disposed of. This policy should align with legal requirements and best practices.

Step 9: Regular Audits

Conduct regular audits of data handling practices to ensure ongoing compliance with privacy and security measures.

Ensuring data privacy and anonymity is an ongoing responsibility throughout the data collection process and beyond. By taking these steps, you demonstrate your commitment to protecting user data and maintaining the trust of your stakeholders.

Data Quality Control

Data quality control is a crucial step in the data collection process to ensure that the acquired dataset is accurate, reliable, and suitable for training a language model. Poor-quality data can adversely affect the performance of the AI system and lead to biased or misleading results. In this section, we will outline the steps to perform data quality control for the collected dataset:

Step 1: Data Inspection

Inspect the collected dataset to get an overview of its contents. This step involves reviewing the data to identify any potential issues, such as missing values, incorrect labels, or data in the wrong format.

Step 2: Remove Duplicate Entries

Check for duplicate entries in the dataset and remove them. Duplicate data can introduce bias and skew the model's training process.

Step 3: Handle Missing Values

Address missing values in the dataset appropriately. Depending on the situation, you can either fill in missing values with sensible defaults, use imputation techniques, or exclude data points with missing values if they are insignificant in number.

Step 4: Validate Labels and Annotations

If your dataset includes labeled data, verify the correctness of labels and annotations. Human errors or misinterpretations during data labeling can affect the model's training and performance.

Step 5: Outlier Detection and Handling

Detect and handle outliers in the dataset. Outliers are data points that deviate significantly from the majority of the data and may affect the model's generalization. You can either remove outliers or transform them to reduce their impact.

Step 6: Bias Detection and Mitigation

Identify and address potential biases in the dataset. Biases in the data can lead to biased AI models, which may result in unfair or discriminatory behavior. Implement techniques to mitigate biases, such as re-sampling or using specialized algorithms.

Step 7: Data Balancing (if applicable)

If your dataset is imbalanced (i.e., some classes have significantly more samples than others), consider balancing the dataset. Techniques like oversampling, undersampling, or generating synthetic data can help balance class distributions and improve model performance.

Step 8: Cross-Validation

Perform cross-validation to evaluate the model's performance on different subsets of the data. This technique helps assess the model's ability to generalize to new, unseen data and avoid overfitting.

Step 9: External Validation

If possible, obtain external validation of the dataset from domain experts or third-party reviewers. External validation can provide valuable insights into the dataset's quality and potential issues that may have been overlooked.

Step 10: Continuous Monitoring

Implement a process for continuous monitoring of the dataset, especially if the data is sourced from dynamic or evolving environments. Regularly update and reevaluate the dataset to ensure it remains relevant and accurate.

By diligently following these steps, you can improve the overall quality of the dataset and create a robust foundation for training a language model that can deliver reliable and insightful results. Data quality control is an ongoing process, and it's essential to revisit and refine these steps whenever new data is collected or data sources change.

Documentation and Metadata

Documentation and metadata play a critical role in ensuring the proper management and understanding of the collected data. In this section, we will outline the steps to create comprehensive documentation and metadata for the dataset:

Step 1: Data Description

Provide a detailed description of the dataset, including its purpose, contents, and intended use. Clearly define the problem the dataset aims to address and how it aligns with the goals and objectives of the AI system.

Step 2: Data Source Information

Document the sources from which the data was obtained. Include information about the origin of the data, any third-party providers, data owners, or organizations involved in the data collection process.

Step 3: Data Collection Process

Explain the process used to collect the data. This should include details on data crawling, data downloading, or any other methods used to gather the dataset. Mention any specific considerations taken to ensure data privacy and compliance with legal requirements.

Step 4: Data Preprocessing

Describe the preprocessing steps applied to the data. This includes any text cleaning, tokenization, normalization, or other transformations performed to prepare the data for modeling.

Step 5: Data Annotations and Labels

If the dataset contains labeled data, provide information on the annotation process. Explain how labels were assigned to data points, the criteria used for labeling, and any guidelines or standards followed during annotation.

Step 6: Data Splits

Document how the dataset is split into training, validation, and test sets. Specify the proportion of data allocated to each set and any considerations made to ensure the sets are representative of the entire dataset.

Step 7: Data Statistics

Include descriptive statistics of the dataset, such as the number of samples, classes, and features. Compute statistical measures like mean, standard deviation, and distribution to gain insights into the dataset's characteristics.

Step 8: Data Format

Specify the format of the data, such as CSV, JSON, or other file types. Provide details on how the data is structured, including the meaning of each column or field.

Step 9: Metadata Schema

Design a metadata schema to capture essential information about each data point. The schema should include relevant attributes like text content, author, date, and any other information pertinent to the dataset.

Step 10: Data Versioning and Updates

Implement a versioning system to keep track of changes made to the dataset over time. Document any updates or revisions to the data and their reasons to maintain a clear historical record.

Step 11: Data Licenses and Usage Rights

Specify the licenses and usage rights associated with the dataset. If the data includes third-party content, ensure compliance with their terms and conditions.

Step 12: Sharing and Access Policies

Define policies for sharing and accessing the dataset. Specify who can access the data, under what conditions, and any restrictions on data distribution.

Step 13: Data Citation

Provide a recommended citation for the dataset to enable proper attribution when others use the data in their research or applications.

By following these steps, you can create comprehensive documentation and metadata that enhance the understanding, transparency, and reproducibility of the dataset. Proper documentation is vital for collaborating with others, publishing research, and ensuring the dataset's long-term usability and impact.

Data collection is a critical step in developing an NLP AI tool for novel writing. By carefully selecting and curating a diverse and representative dataset, you provide the foundation for training a robust and effective NLP model.

DATA COLLECTION

3.

Preprocessing

Clean and preprocess the text data by removing unnecessary characters, punctuation, and formatting inconsistencies. Normalize the text to ensure consistency across the dataset.

Preprocessing is an essential step in creating a natural language processing (NLP) AI for novel writing. It involves cleaning and preparing the text data to ensure consistency and remove unnecessary noise. Here's a detailed explanation of the steps involved:

Text Cleaning

Text cleaning is a crucial preprocessing step in natural language processing (NLP) that involves removing noise and irrelevant information from the text data. In this section, we will outline the step-by-step process of text cleaning:

Step 1: Convert to Lowercase

Convert the entire text to lowercase to ensure consistency in the text data. This step prevents the model from treating the same word in different cases as different words.

```python
# Example Python code for converting text to lowercase
text = "Hello World!"
cleaned_text = text.lower()
print(cleaned_text)  # Output: "hello world!"
```

Step 2: Remove Special Characters

Remove any special characters, such as punctuation, symbols, or non-alphanumeric characters, from the text. These characters usually do not contribute much to the meaning and can be safely removed.

```python
# Example Python code for removing special characters
import re

text = "Hello, World!"
cleaned_text = re.sub(r'[^\w\s]', '', text)
print(cleaned_text)  # Output: "Hello World"
```

Step 3: Remove Numbers

If the presence of numbers is not essential for your NLP task, you can remove them from the text.

```python
```

```python
# Example Python code for removing numbers
import re

text = "Hello123 World456"
cleaned_text = re.sub(r'\d', '', text)
print(cleaned_text)   # Output: "Hello World"
```

Step 4: Remove Extra Whitespace

Remove any extra whitespace or newline characters from the text. This step ensures that the text is well-formatted and easy to process.

```python
# Example Python code for removing extra whitespace
text = "   Hello    World   "
cleaned_text = " ".join(text.split())
print(cleaned_text)   # Output: "Hello World"
```

Step 5: Handle Contractions (Optional)

Depending on the NLP task, you may choose to handle contractions. For example, you can expand contractions like "don't" to "do not" to avoid any ambiguity.

```python
# Example Python code for handling contractions (optional)
import contractions

text = "I don't like this."
cleaned_text = contractions.fix(text)
print(cleaned_text)   # Output: "I do not like this."
```

Step 6: Remove Stopwords (Optional)

Depending on your NLP task, you might want to remove common stopwords (e.g., "the," "is," "and") as they often do not carry significant meaning.

```python
C# Example Python code for removing stopwords (optional)
from nltk.corpus import stopwords
from nltk.tokenize import word_tokenize

text = "This is an example sentence."
stop_words = set(stopwords.words('english'))
words = word_tokenize(text)
cleaned_text = " ".join([word for word in words if word.
```

PREPROCESSING

```
lower() not in stop_words])
print(cleaned_text)  # Output: "example sentence"
```

Step 7: Lemmatization or Stemming (Optional)

You can choose to perform lemmatization or stemming to reduce words to their base or root form, respectively. This helps in further reducing the vocabulary size and keeping only the essential information.

```python
Copy code# Example Python code for lemmatization (optional)#
Example Python code for lemmatization (optional)
from nltk.stem import WordNetLemmatizer

text = "running dogs jumped over fences"
lemmatizer = WordNetLemmatizer()
words = word_tokenize(text)
cleaned_text = " ".join([lemmatizer.lemmatize(word) for word in words])
print(cleaned_text)  # Output: "running dog jumped over fence"
```

By following these text cleaning steps, you can ensure that your text data is prepared and ready for further preprocessing and training the language model for the NLP tasks in your AI system.

Tokenization

Tokenization is the process of breaking down the text into smaller units called tokens. These tokens can be words, subwords, or even characters. Tokenization makes it easier to process and analyze the text at a more granular level.

Tokenization is a critical preprocessing step in natural language processing (NLP) that involves breaking down the text into smaller units, usually words or subwords, known as tokens. In this section, we will outline the step-by-step process of text tokenization:

Step 1: Sentence Tokenization

Before tokenizing words, it is common to perform sentence tokenization, which involves splitting the text into individual sentences. The goal is to break down the text into meaningful units to process each sentence separately.

```python
# Example Python code for sentence tokenization
import nltk

text = "This is the first sentence. This is the second sentence."
sentences = nltk.sent_tokenize(text)
print(sentences)
# Output: ['This is the first sentence.', 'This is the second sentence.']
```

Step 2: Word Tokenization

Word tokenization involves splitting each sentence into individual words. This step helps in preparing the text for further analysis, such as counting words or applying machine learning algorithms.

```python
# Example Python code for word tokenization
from nltk.tokenize import word_tokenize

sentence = "This is the first sentence."
words = word_tokenize(sentence)
print(words)
# Output: ['This', 'is', 'the', 'first', 'sentence', '.']
```

Step 3: Subword Tokenization (Optional)

PREPROCESSING

In some cases, it might be beneficial to tokenize the text into subwords instead of words. Subword tokenization can handle out-of-vocabulary words and can be particularly useful in languages with complex word formations.

```python
# Example Python code for subword tokenization (using SentencePiece)
import sentencepiece as spm

text = "This is the first sentence. This is the second sentence."
# Train a SentencePiece model on the text data
spm.SentencePieceTrainer.Train('--input=data.txt --model_prefix=m --vocab_size=500')
# Load the trained SentencePiece model
sp = spm.SentencePieceProcessor(model_file='m.model')
tokens = sp.EncodeAsPieces(text)
print(tokens)
# Output: ['▁This', '▁is', '▁the', '▁first', '▁sentence',
'.', '▁This', '▁is', '▁the', '▁second', '▁sentence', '.']
```

Step 4: Custom Tokenization Rules (Optional)

In some cases, you may need to apply custom tokenization rules based on specific requirements of your NLP task. For example, you might want to keep certain phrases together as a single token.

```python
# Example Python code for custom tokenization rules
import re

text = "Let's analyze this text."
# Custom tokenization to handle contractions
tokens = re.findall(r'\w+|[\w\']+', text)
print(tokens)
# Output: ["Let's", 'analyze', 'this', 'text']
```

By following these tokenization steps, you can effectively break down the text into meaningful units (words or subwords) and prepare it for further preprocessing and training your language model for the NLP tasks in your AI system.

67

Stopword Removal

Stopwords are commonly used words in a language that do not carry significant meaning, such as "and," "the," or "is." Removing stopwords can help reduce noise and improve the efficiency of downstream tasks. Stopword removal is typically performed using predefined lists or language-specific libraries.

Stopword removal is a crucial step in natural language processing (NLP) preprocessing, where common words with little contextual meaning are eliminated from the text. These words, known as stopwords, include articles, prepositions, and other frequently occurring words. Removing stopwords can help reduce noise in the data and improve the efficiency of downstream tasks, such as text classification or sentiment analysis.

Step-by-step instructions for stopword removal:

Step 1: Identify the Stopwords List

First, you need to create or obtain a list of stopwords specific to the language you are processing. Many NLP libraries, such as NLTK for Python, provide predefined lists of stopwords for various languages.

```python
# Example Python code to obtain the list of stopwords for
English using NLTK
import nltk
nltk.download('stopwords')
from nltk.corpus import stopwords

stopwords_list = set(stopwords.words('english'))
```

Step 2: Tokenization

Before removing stopwords, you need to tokenize the text into individual words or tokens. You can use the same tokenization techniques discussed in section 3.2.

```python
# Tokenization code (assuming the 'text' variable contains
the input text)
from nltk.tokenize import word_tokenize

tokens = word_tokenize(text)
```

Step 3: Stopword Removal

PREPROCESSING

Now, you can remove the stopwords from the tokenized text using the stopwords list obtained in **Step 1**.

```python
# Example Python code for stopword removal
filtered_tokens = [word for word in tokens if word.lower()
not in stopwords_list]
```

Step 4: Reconstruct the Text

After removing stopwords, you might want to reconstruct the text to perform further analysis or feed it into your language model.

```python
# Example Python code to reconstruct the text after stopword removal
filtered_text = ' '.join(filtered_tokens)
print(filtered_text)
```

By following these steps, you can effectively remove common stopwords from the text data, making it cleaner and more suitable for various NLP tasks. Keep in mind that the list of stopwords can be customized based on the specific requirements of your NLP project. Additionally, the choice of stopwords may vary depending on the domain or context of the text data being processed.

Lowercasing

Lowercasing is a common preprocessing step in natural language processing (NLP) where all the text in the input document is converted to lowercase. This step is essential for ensuring uniformity and consistency in the text data, as it helps in treating the same word with different cases as the same word, regardless of whether it appears in uppercase or lowercase.

Step-by-step instructions for lowercasing:

Step 1: Load the Text Data

First, you need to load the text data that you want to preprocess. This data could be in the form of a string, a text file, or a collection of text documents.

Step 2: Convert Text to Lowercase

Next, you can use the programming language's built-in functions or libraries to convert the text to lowercase. The method for converting text to lowercase may vary depending on the programming language you are using. Below are examples of how to do this in Python and JavaScript:

Python:

```python
# Example Python code for lowercasing text
text = "This is an Example Text"
lowercased_text = text.lower()
print(lowercased_text)
```

JavaScript:

```javascript
// Example JavaScript code for lowercasing text
let text = "This is an Example Text";
let lowercasedText = text.toLowerCase();
console.log(lowercasedText);
```

Step 3: Reassign or Save the Lowercased Text

After converting the text to lowercase, you can choose to reassign the lowercased text to the original variable or save it to a new variable for further processing.

Step 4: Continue with Further Preprocessing

Once the text has been converted to lowercase, you can proceed with other preprocessing steps, such as tokenization, stopword removal, lemmatization, and more, as mentioned in other sections of the book.

Lowercasing is a simple but crucial step in text preprocessing, as it ensures consistency in the text data, which can significantly impact the accuracy and performance of NLP models. However, it's important to note that in some cases, you may want to preserve the case of specific words (e.g., proper nouns) based on the requirements of your NLP task. In such cases, it's essential to handle the lowercasing process carefully and selectively.

Lemmatization or Stemming

Lemmatization and stemming are techniques used to reduce words to their base or root form. Lemmatization aims to reduce words to their dictionary or canonical form (lemmas), while stemming truncates words to their stem form by removing prefixes or suffixes. These techniques help consolidate variations of words and reduce vocabulary size.

Lemmatization and stemming are two common text preprocessing techniques used in Natural Language Processing (NLP) to reduce words to their base or root form. The goal of both techniques is to normalize words so that variations of the same word are treated as a single entity, which can improve the efficiency and effectiveness of NLP tasks such as text classification and information retrieval.

Lemmatization: Lemmatization is the process of reducing words to their base or root form, known as the lemma. The lemma represents the canonical form of a word and is linguistically meaningful. For example, the lemma of the words "running," "runs," and "ran" is "run." Lemmatization involves considering the context and meaning of the word to perform the normalization accurately.

Step-by-step instructions for Lemmatization:

Step 1: Load the Text Data

First, you need to load the text data that you want to preprocess. This data could be in the form of a string, a text file, or a collection of text documents.

Step 2: Tokenization

Before lemmatizing the text, you need to tokenize it into individual words. Tokenization is the process of splitting the text into words or tokens.

Step 3: Lemmatization using NLP Libraries

There are several NLP libraries that offer lemmatization capabilities. One popular library is NLTK (Natural Language Toolkit) in Python.

Here's an example of lemmatization using NLTK in Python:

```python
import nltk
from nltk.stem import WordNetLemmatizer
nltk.download('wordnet')

# Sample text
text = "The quick brown foxes are running."
```

PREPROCESSING

```
# Tokenize the text
words = nltk.word_tokenize(text)

# Initialize the WordNetLemmatizer
lemmatizer = WordNetLemmatizer()

# Lemmatize the words
lemmatized_words = [lemmatizer.lemmatize(word) for word in words]

print(lemmatized_words)
```

Output: ['The', 'quick', 'brown', 'fox', 'are', 'running', '.']

Stemming: Stemming is a simpler version of normalization that removes suffixes from words to obtain their root form, known as the stem. The stem may or may not be a valid word, but it represents the core meaning of the original word. For example, stemming would reduce the words "running," "runs," and "ran" to the stem "run."

Step-by-step instructions for Stemming:

Step 1: Load the Text Data

First, you need to load the text data that you want to preprocess. This data could be in the form of a string, a text file, or a collection of text documents.

Step 2: Tokenization

Before stemming the text, you need to tokenize it into individual words. Tokenization is the process of splitting the text into words or tokens.

Step 3: Stemming using NLP Libraries

There are several NLP libraries that offer stemming capabilities. One popular library is NLTK (Natural Language Toolkit) in Python.

Here's an example of stemming using NLTK in Python:

```python
Copy codeimport nltkfrom nltk.stem import PorterStemmernltk.
import nltk
from nltk.stem import PorterStemmer
nltk.download('punkt')

# Sample text
text = "The quick brown foxes are running."

# Tokenize the text
words = nltk.word_tokenize(text)
```

73

```
# Initialize the PorterStemmer
stemmer = PorterStemmer()

# Stem the words
stemmed_words = [stemmer.stem(word) for word in words]

print(stemmed_words)
```

Output: ['the', 'quick', 'brown', 'fox', 'are', 'run', '.']

Both lemmatization and stemming help in reducing words to their base forms, but lemmatization generally produces more linguistically accurate results as it considers the context and meaning of the words. However, stemming is faster and can be sufficient for certain applications where linguistic accuracy is not the primary concern. The choice between lemmatization and stemming depends on the specific requirements and constraints of your NLP task.

Removing Punctuation

Remove punctuation marks from the text data. Punctuation marks such as commas, periods, and quotation marks are often unnecessary for many NLP tasks and can be safely removed without losing crucial information.

Punctuation marks in text can be noisy and may not always be essential for certain NLP tasks. Removing punctuation is a common preprocessing step to simplify the text data and reduce the number of distinct tokens that the NLP model needs to process.

Step-by-step instructions for Removing Punctuation:

Step 1: Load the Text Data

First, you need to load the text data that you want to preprocess. This data could be in the form of a string, a text file, or a collection of text documents.

Step 2: Text Cleaning (Optional)

Before removing punctuation, you may want to perform text cleaning, which involves tasks such as removing special characters, extra whitespace, and handling encoding issues. Depending on the quality of your data, this step can help ensure better results in subsequent preprocessing steps.

Step 3: Remove Punctuation

To remove punctuation from the text, you can use regular expressions or string operations in Python.

Using Regular Expressions:

```python
import re

def remove_punctuation(text):
    # Define a regular expression pattern to match punctuation
    # \W matches any non-word character (punctuation, symbols, etc.)
    # \s matches whitespace characters (space, tab, newline, etc.)
    # \d matches digits
    # Combine all into one pattern using square brackets []
    pattern = r"[^\w\s\d]"

    # Use the re.sub() function to replace matches with an empty string
    # This effectively removes all punctuation from the text
    cleaned_text = re.sub(pattern, "", text)
    return cleaned_text
```

```
# Sample text
text = "Hello, world! This is an example text with
punctuation."

# Remove punctuation
cleaned_text = remove_punctuation(text)

print(cleaned_text)
```

Output: "Hello world This is an example text with punctuation"

Using String Operations:

```python
def remove_punctuation(text):
    # Define a string containing all punctuation marks
    punctuation_marks = '''!()-[]{};:'"\,<>./?@#$%^&*_~'''

    # Use the str.translate() function to remove punctuation
    cleaned_text = text.translate(str.maketrans('', '', punctuation_marks))
    return cleaned_text

# Sample text
text = "Hello, world! This is an example text with
punctuation."

# Remove punctuation
cleaned_text = remove_punctuation(text)

print(cleaned_text)
```

Output: "Hello world This is an example text with punctuation"

It is important to note that removing punctuation can sometimes lead to the loss of important information, especially in tasks like sentiment analysis or emotion detection, where punctuation can carry meaningful cues. Therefore, consider the nature of your NLP task before deciding to remove punctuation entirely. Additionally, if your NLP task requires preserving certain punctuation marks, you can customize the list of punctuation_marks accordingly.

Handling Special Cases

Address any special cases specific to your dataset or requirements. For example, you may want to handle contractions (e.g., "don't" to "do not"), correct spelling errors, or handle specific domain-related terminology.

In natural language processing (NLP), special cases refer to specific instances or patterns in the text data that require unique handling. These cases often involve words or phrases that might not follow the regular grammatical rules or could be crucial for the context of the NLP task. Handling special cases is important to ensure that the NLP model can effectively process and understand such instances in the text.

Step-by-step instructions for Handling Special Cases:

Step 1: Identify Special Cases

The first step is to identify the special cases present in your text data. These may include:

a) Proper nouns: Names of people, places, or organizations that should be preserved with their original capitalization.

b) Acronyms: Abbreviations formed by taking the initial letters of a phrase, which need to be kept intact.

c) Numbers and dates: Numerical expressions that may require specific processing based on the NLP task.

Step 2: Define Rules for Special Cases

Once you have identified the special cases, you need to define rules for handling them appropriately. For instance:

a) Proper nouns: Preserve the capitalization of proper nouns by excluding them from lowercasing processes.

b) Acronyms: Identify acronyms and ensure they are not subjected to tokenization, splitting, or any modification.

c) Numbers and dates: Decide whether you want to convert numbers to their word representation (e.g., "25" to "twenty-five") or keep them as numerical values.

Step 3: Implement Special Case Handling

Depending on the programming language or NLP library you are using, you can implement special case handling using conditional statements or regular expressions.

Example in Python:

```python
import re

def handle_special_cases(text):
    # Define a list of proper nouns
    proper_nouns = ["John", "New York", "OpenAI", ...]
    
    # Define a regular expression pattern for identifying acronyms (assuming they are all uppercase)
    acronym_pattern = r'\b[A-Z]{2,}\b'
    
    # Use the re.sub() function to apply rules for special cases
    # For proper nouns, we simply preserve the original capitalization
    for proper_noun in proper_nouns:
        text = re.sub(r'\b{}\b'.format(proper_noun), proper_noun, text)
    
    # For acronyms, we ensure they are not affected by tokenization
    text = re.sub(acronym_pattern, lambda match: match.group().replace(" ", "_"), text)
    
    # Handle other special cases as needed based on your defined rules
    
    return text

# Sample text
text = "The company OpenAI, based in New York, is known for its NLP advancements."

# Handle special cases
processed_text = handle_special_cases(text)

print(processed_text)
```

Output: "The company OpenAI, based in New York, is known for its NLP advancements."

In this example, we preserved the capitalization of the proper noun "OpenAI" and ensured that the acronym "NLP" remains intact by replacing spaces with underscores during preprocessing.

Remember that the specific rules for handling special cases may vary depending on the nature of your NLP task and the requirements of your dataset. Always validate the results to ensure the special cases are correctly handled in your text data.

PREPROCESSING

Normalization

Normalize the text to ensure consistency and improve generalization. Normalization involves standardizing features such as dates, numbers, and abbreviations. For example, converting "12th" to "twelfth" or "100%" to "one hundred percent."

Normalization is an essential step in the preprocessing of text data for natural language processing (NLP) tasks. The goal of normalization is to transform the text into a standard and consistent format, which can help improve the accuracy and effectiveness of NLP models. Normalization involves converting text to a common representation, such as converting contractions to their full forms, expanding abbreviations, and handling other linguistic variations.

Step-by-step instructions for Normalization:

Step 1: Create a Normalization Map

Start by creating a normalization map, which contains the common variations of words and their corresponding normalized forms. This map can be manually constructed or can be based on existing libraries and resources.

Example normalization map:

python

Copy codenormalization_map = { "isn't": "is not", "don't": "do not", "couldn't": "could not", "won't": "will not", # Add more entries as needed}
Step 2: Implement Normalization FunctionNext, implement a function that performs the normalization based on the normalization map. The function will replace the variations in the text with their normalized forms.

Example in Python:

```python
import re

def normalize_text(text, normalization_map):
    # Use regular expressions to match and replace variations in the text
    for variation, normalized_form in normalization_map.items():
        pattern = re.compile(r'\b{}\b'.format(re.escape(variation)), re.IGNORECASE)
        text = re.sub(pattern, normalized_form, text)

    return text
```

PREPROCESSING

```
# Sample text
text = "He couldn't believe that she isn't coming. Don't you
think it won't matter?"

# Normalize the text
normalized_text = normalize_text(text, normalization_map)

print(normalized_text)
```

Output: "He could not believe that she is not coming. Do not you think it will not matter?"

In this example, we used the normalization map to convert contractions like "couldn't" to "could not," "isn't" to "is not," and "don't" to "do not."

Step 3: Additional Normalization Techniques

Depending on your specific NLP task and the characteristics of your text data, you might consider other normalization techniques such as:

a) Expanding abbreviations: Convert abbreviations like "Mr." to "Mister" or "Dr." to "Doctor."

b) Removing special characters: Eliminate special characters, punctuation, or symbols that are not relevant to the NLP task.

c) Handling numerical expressions: Normalize numbers to a common format or replace them with their word representation.

Remember that the normalization process should be tailored to the requirements of your NLP task and the characteristics of your dataset. Regularly validate the results to ensure that the text is transformed correctly and consistently.`

Text Formatting

Apply appropriate text formatting techniques based on your needs. This may involve removing excessive whitespace, handling line breaks or paragraphs, or ensuring consistent sentence or paragraph lengths.

Text formatting is a crucial step in the preprocessing of text data for natural language processing (NLP) tasks. Proper text formatting ensures that the text is in a consistent and standardized layout, which can facilitate better model performance and readability.

Step-by-step instructions for Text Formatting:

Step 1: Remove Unnecessary Whitespace

Remove any extra spaces or tabs from the text, as they do not carry meaningful information and can interfere with NLP tasks.

Example in Python:

```python
def remove_extra_whitespace(text):
    return ' '.join(text.split())
```

Step 2: Sentence Segmentation

Segment the text into individual sentences, as this can be useful for certain NLP tasks such as sentiment analysis and text summarization.

Example in Python using NLTK:

```python
import nltk
def sentence_segmentation(text):
    sentences = nltk.sent_tokenize(text)
    return sentences
```

Step 3: Paragraph Segmentation

Segment the text into paragraphs, as it may be relevant for certain NLP tasks, such as document summarization.

Example in Python:

```python
```

PREPROCESSING

```
def paragraph_segmentation(text):
    paragraphs = text.split('\n\n')
    # Assuming paragraphs are separated by two newlines
    return paragraphs
```

Step 4: Capitalization

Decide on the appropriate capitalization for your NLP task. In some cases, you may want to preserve the original capitalization, while in others, you might choose to convert all text to lowercase for better generalization.

Example in Python:

```python
def lowercase_text(text):
    return text.lower()
```

Step 5: Numeric Values

Decide how to handle numeric values in the text. You may choose to convert all numbers to a generic representation (e.g., "NUM") or retain the specific numeric values.

Step 6: Special Characters

Consider how to deal with special characters or symbols. Depending on your NLP task, you might choose to remove them or replace them with relevant information.

Step 7: Date and Time Formats

If your text contains date and time information, consider standardizing their representation to a common format for consistency.

Remember that the text formatting process should be tailored to the specific requirements of your NLP task and the characteristics of your dataset. Regularly validate the results to ensure that the text is formatted correctly and appropriately for your chosen NLP model or application.

By performing these preprocessing steps, you can transform raw text data into a cleaner and more standardized format, which is easier to analyze and feed into the subsequent stages of your NLP AI pipeline.

Keep in mind that the specific preprocessing steps may vary based on the characteristics of your dataset and the requirements of your novel writing tool. Experimentation and exploration of the dataset will help you determine the most effective preprocessing techniques for your particular use case.

4. Training a Language Model

You can utilize existing NLP frameworks like TensorFlow, PyTorch, or Hugging Face's Transformers to train your language model. Train the model using techniques such as recurrent neural networks (RNNs), long short-term memory (LSTM), or transformer models like GPT (Generative Pre-trained Transformer).

Training a language model is a crucial step in creating your natural language processing (NLP) AI for novel writing. It involves utilizing existing NLP frameworks like TensorFlow, PyTorch, or Hugging Face's Transformers to train a language model. Here's a detailed explanation of the steps involved:

Selecting a Base Model

Start by selecting a suitable base model that will serve as the foundation for your novel writing AI. Popular choices include transformer models like GPT (Generative Pre-trained Transformer) or recurrent neural networks (RNNs) such as LSTM (Long Short-Term Memory). These models are designed to capture the underlying structure and patterns in text data.

Selecting an appropriate base model is a crucial step in crafting an effective language model for natural language processing (NLP) tasks. The choice of the base model depends on factors such as the complexity of the NLP task, the size of the dataset, available computational resources, and the desired level of performance. In this section, we will explore the process of selecting a suitable base model for your NLP project.

Step-by-step instructions for Selecting a Base Model:

Step 1: Understand NLP Task Requirements

Before selecting a base model, thoroughly understand the requirements of your NLP task. Determine the specific task you want the language model to perform, such as text classification, named entity recognition, machine translation, or text generation.

Step 2: Review Existing Pre-trained Models

Review the landscape of existing pre-trained language models and their performance on similar NLP tasks. Popular base models include BERT, GPT (and its variants), RoBERTa, XLNet, and others. Consider recent research papers and model benchmarks to identify state-of-the-art models for your task.

Step 3: Consider Model Size and Complexity

Assess the size and complexity of the base models in relation to your available computational resources. Larger models with more parameters generally provide better performance but require more memory and processing power.

Step 4: Evaluate Computational Cost

Estimate the computational cost of training and fine-tuning the base models. Consider factors such as training time, hardware requirements, and memory constraints. If you have limited computational resources, consider using smaller or more efficient models.

Step 5: Check Availability of Pre-trained Models

Ensure that the selected base model is available in a pre-trained format. Many popular NLP models are available for download with pre-trained weights and can be further fine-tuned for specific tasks.

Step 6: Explore Transfer Learning

Consider the potential of transfer learning. Transfer learning involves using a pre-trained base model and fine-tuning it on your specific dataset. This approach leverages the knowledge captured by the base model from a large corpus of data, which can be beneficial when you have a limited dataset.

Step 7: Fine-tuning Capabilities

Evaluate the fine-tuning capabilities of the base model. Some models are designed with specific architectures for efficient fine-tuning and adaptation to downstream tasks.

Step 8: Experiment and Compare

Conduct experiments with different base models and fine-tuning approaches. Train and validate each model on your dataset and compare their performance metrics such as accuracy, F1 score, or perplexity. Choose the model that best suits your task and dataset.

Step 9: Document the Selection Process

Document the entire process of selecting the base model, including the reasoning behind your choice. This documentation will be valuable for future reference and for sharing insights with your team or stakeholders.

Remember that the selection of a base model can significantly impact the success of your NLP project. Take the time to carefully assess your needs, explore available options, and conduct experiments to identify the most suitable base model for your specific task.

Data Preparation

Prepare your novel text dataset for training. This involves organizing the data into a format suitable for the chosen NLP framework. Typically, the data is split into sequences or chunks of text, and the model is trained to predict the next word or sequence given the previous context. The dataset should cover a wide range of novel genres, writing styles, and themes to ensure the model's generalization capabilities.

Data preparation is a critical step in training a language model for natural language processing (NLP) tasks. It involves transforming raw text data into a format suitable for input into the language model. In this section, we will walk through the process of data preparation for training a language model.

Step-by-step instructions for Data Preparation:

Step 1: Data Cleaning and Text Preprocessing

Before preparing the data, ensure that the raw text data is cleaned and pre-processed. This step includes tasks such as removing special characters, handling missing values, correcting spelling errors, and handling any other data-specific issues. Refer to Section 3.1 ("Text Cleaning") for detailed text cleaning techniques.

Step 2: Splitting into Train and Validation Sets

Divide the preprocessed data into two sets: the training set and the validation set. The training set will be used to train the language model, while the validation set will be used to monitor the model's performance and prevent overfitting during training.

Step 3: Tokenization

Tokenization is the process of breaking down text into individual tokens, which could be words, subwords, or characters. Most language models require tokenized input. Use a tokenizer to split the text into tokens and assign unique numerical IDs to each token. Common libraries for tokenization include Hugging Face's transformers library (https://github.com/huggingface/transformers) and TensorFlow's Tokenizer class.

Step 4: Encoding and Embedding

After tokenization, convert the tokenized sequences into numerical representations that can be fed into the language model. This process is known as encoding. The encoder maps tokens to their corresponding IDs and converts them into numerical tensors. Embedding is the process of representing each token with a dense vector of fixed dimensions. These embeddings capture semantic meaning and are learned during the training process. Libraries like TensorFlow and PyTorch provide built-in functions for encoding and embedding.

Step 5: Padding and Batch Creation

Language models typically require inputs to have a consistent length. If the text sequences have varying lengths, pad or truncate them to a fixed length. Padding involves adding special tokens (usually 0) to the shorter sequences to make them equal in length. Divide the data into batches to facilitate efficient training. Batch sizes depend on the available memory and processing capabilities of your hardware.

Step 6: Create Input and Output Tensors

Define the input and output tensors for the language model. In most cases, the language model follows an autoregressive approach, where the output at each time step is predicted based on the previous time steps. Thus, the input tensor will be the tokenized sequence, and the output tensor will be shifted by one token ahead of the input tensor.

Step 7: Data Loading

Create data loaders or generators that efficiently load batches of data during training. Data loading is crucial for optimizing the training process and minimizing I/O bottlenecks.

Step 8: Save Prepared Data

Save the preprocessed and prepared data in a format that can be easily loaded during model training. Common formats include binary files or serialized objects. This step ensures that the prepared data can be reused and shared among team members.

By following these steps, you will have a well-prepared dataset ready for training the language model. Remember that the quality and efficiency of the data preparation process significantly impact the model's performance and training speed. Carefully clean and preprocess the data, tokenize and encode the text, and create batches to facilitate smooth model training.

Tokenization

Tokenization is the process of breaking down the text into smaller units or tokens, such as words or subwords, to facilitate the training process. Each token is assigned a unique numerical representation, allowing the model to process and learn from the text data. NLP frameworks often provide built-in tokenization methods that you can use.

Tokenization is a crucial step in the data preparation process for training a language model. It involves breaking down raw text data into individual tokens, which could be words, subwords, or characters. Tokenization is necessary because language models operate on discrete units (tokens) rather than raw text. In this section, we will explore the tokenization process in detail.

Step-by-step instructions for Tokenization:

Step 1: Choose a Tokenization Library

Select a tokenization library that suits your specific language model and NLP task. Commonly used tokenization libraries include Hugging Face's transformers library (https://github.com/huggingface/transformers) for popular pre-trained language models, and NLTK (Natural Language Toolkit) for basic tokenization in Python.

Step 2: Load the Data

Load the preprocessed text data that you prepared in Section 3 ("Preprocessing"). Ensure that the text data is clean and free from any special characters or irrelevant content.

Step 3: Initialize the Tokenizer

Initialize the tokenizer from the chosen library. If you are using the Hugging Face transformers library, you can load a pre-trained tokenizer for the specific language model you are using. For example, for the GPT-2 model:

```python
Copy codefrom transformers import GPT2Tokenizer# Load the GPT-2 tokenizertokenizer = GPT2Tokenizer.from_pretrained("gpt2")
```

Step 4: Tokenize the Text

Use the initialized tokenizer to tokenize the text data. The tokenizer will break the text into individual tokens and provide a mapping from tokens to their corresponding numerical IDs. Different tokenization libraries may have slightly different methods for tokenization.

```python
# Tokenize the text
tokenized_data = tokenizer.encode("your input text goes here")
```

Step 5: Handling Special Tokens

Some language models require special tokens, such as a "start of sequence" token, an "end of sequence" token, and a padding token. These tokens are used for various purposes, such as denoting the beginning and end of a sequence or filling sequences to a fixed length. Make sure to add these special tokens to the tokenized data if your language model requires them.

```python
# Add special tokens if needed
tokenized_data = tokenizer.encode("your input text goes here", add_special_tokens=True)
```

Step 6: Handling Maximum Length

Some language models have a maximum sequence length that they can handle due to memory limitations. Check the maximum token length supported by your language model and truncate or pad the tokenized data accordingly.

```python
# Truncate or pad the tokenized data to a maximum length
max_length = 512  # Replace with your model's maximum length
tokenized_data = tokenized_data[:max_length] + [tokenizer.pad_token_id] * (max_length - len(tokenized_data))
```

Step 7: Batch Tokenization

If you are dealing with a large dataset, it is often more efficient to tokenize the data in batches. This can be achieved using the tokenizer.batch_encode_plus() method in the transformers library.

```python
batch_sentences = ["sentence 1", "sentence 2", ...]
batch_tokenized = tokenizer.batch_encode_plus(batch_sentences, add_special_tokens=True, padding=True,
```

By following these steps, you have successfully tokenized your raw text data, and it is now ready for encoding and embedding in the next steps of the data preparation process. Tokenization is an essential step in NLP tasks, as it transforms raw text data into a format that can be effectively processed by language models.

Encoding and Embedding

Convert the tokens into numerical representations that can be understood by the model. This step involves encoding the tokens as numerical vectors or embeddings. Word embeddings capture the semantic relationships between words, allowing the model to understand the context and meaning of the text.

Once the text data has been tokenized, the next step in the data preparation process for training a language model is to convert the tokenized data into numerical representations. This process involves encoding the tokens and generating embeddings, which are dense vector representations of the tokens that capture their semantic meaning. In this section, we will explore the encoding and embedding process in detail.

Step-by-step instructions for Encoding and Embedding:

Step 1: Initialize the Language Model

Choose a pre-trained language model that suits your NLP task and load it using a library like Hugging Face's transformers.

```python
from transformers import GPT2Tokenizer, GPT2Model

# Load the pre-trained GPT-2 tokenizer and model
tokenizer = GPT2Tokenizer.from_pretrained("gpt2")
model = GPT2Model.from_pretrained("gpt2")
```

Step 2: Prepare Tokenized Data

Ensure that the tokenized data is formatted in a way that can be easily fed into the language model. For example, convert the tokenized data into a PyTorch tensor or a NumPy array.

```python
import torch

# Example tokenized data
tokenized_data = [101, 3209, 2003, 2009, 1037, 2485, 1010, 102]
# Convert tokenized data to PyTorch tensor
input_ids = torch.tensor(tokenized_data).unsqueeze(0)  # Add batch dimension
```

Step 3: Encode the TokensPass the tokenized data through the language model to obtain encoded representations of the tokens. These representations are often referred to as hidden states or contextual embeddings.

```python
# Forward pass through the model
outputs = model(input_ids)
# Get the hidden states (last layer) from the model outputs
hidden_states = outputs.last_hidden_state
```

Step 4: Extract Token Embeddings

The hidden states contain embeddings for all tokens in the input sequence. However, for most NLP tasks, we are only interested in the embedding of a specific token, such as the last token representing the end of the sequence or the [CLS] token in BERT-based models.

```python
# Example: Get the embedding of the last token
last_token_embedding = hidden_states[:, -1, :]
```

Step 5: Pooling Strategy (Optional)

Depending on the NLP task, you might need to apply a pooling strategy to obtain a fixed-size representation of the entire sequence. Common pooling strategies include mean pooling, max pooling, or using the embedding of a specific token.

```python
# Example: Mean pooling to get a fixed-size representation
of the entire sequence
mean_pooled_embedding = hidden_states.mean(dim=1)
```

Step 6: Using the Embeddings

The embeddings obtained from the language model can now be used for various downstream NLP tasks, such as text classification, sentiment analysis, or language generation.

```python
# Example: Use the embeddings for text classification
```

```
# Assuming you have a classification head on top of the
language model
classification_output = classification_head(mean_pooled_
embedding)
```

By following these steps, you have successfully encoded and embedded the tokenized text data using a pre-trained language model. The embeddings can now be used as inputs for downstream NLP tasks or as feature representations for other machine learning models.

Model Architecture

Define the architecture of your language model. This includes specifying the number of layers, hidden units, attention mechanisms (for transformer models), and other hyperparameters. The architecture determines the capacity and complexity of the model, influencing its ability to learn and generate coherent novel text.

Selecting an appropriate model architecture is a crucial step in training a language model. The architecture determines the structure and complexity of the neural network that will be used to process and understand the language data. In this section, we will explore the process of choosing a model architecture and understanding its components.

Step-by-step instructions for Model Architecture:

Step 1: Research Existing Model Architectures

Before selecting a model architecture, it's essential to research and understand the existing options. There are several pre-trained language models available, each with its strengths and weaknesses. Commonly used architectures include GPT (Generative Pre-trained Transformer), BERT (Bidirectional Encoder Representations from Transformers), and LSTM (Long Short-Term Memory) networks. Consider the requirements of your NLP task, such as sequence length, context, and memory, to choose the most suitable architecture.

Step 2: Hugging Face Transformers Library

Hugging Face's transformers library is a valuable resource for accessing pre-trained language models and their architectures. It provides a wide range of popular models and allows you to load them easily.

```python
from transformers import GPT2Model, GPT2Config

# Load a pre-trained GPT-2 model and configuration
model_name = "gpt2"   # Example: GPT-2
config = GPT2Config.from_pretrained(model_name)
model = GPT2Model.from_pretrained(model_name, config=config)
```

Step 3: Model Configuration

Each model architecture has specific configuration parameters that can be modified to suit your needs. For instance, you can adjust the number of layers, hidden units, attention heads, and other hyperparameters.

```python
# Example: Modify the number of layers in the GPT-2 model
config.num_hidden_layers = 12
```

Step 4: Understanding Model Components

It's crucial to understand the components of the chosen architecture. For instance, the GPT-2 model is based on the Transformer architecture, which includes self-attention mechanisms and feed-forward neural networks in its encoder layers. Understanding these components will help you interpret the model's behavior and make informed decisions during fine-tuning.

Step 5: Visualization (Optional)

Visualizing the model architecture can be helpful in gaining a deeper understanding of its structure. Tools like TensorBoard can be used to plot the model's graph and visualize the connections between different layers.

```python
from torch.utils.tensorboard import SummaryWriter

# Initialize a TensorBoard writer
writer = SummaryWriter()

# Write the model graph to TensorBoard
writer.add_graph(model, input_to_model=inputs)

# Close the writer when done
writer.close()
```

Step 6: Save the Modified Configuration

If you make changes to the model configuration, it's a good practice to save the modified configuration to a file. This will ensure that you can load the same configuration when fine-tuning or using the model later.

```python
# Save the modified configuration to a file
config.save_pretrained("custom_gpt2_config")
```

By following these steps, you can select an appropriate model architecture for your NLP task and understand its components. Remember that the choice of model architecture can significantly impact the performance and efficiency of your language model, so invest time in evaluating and experimenting with different architectures based on your specific needs.

Training Process

Train the language model using your prepared dataset and the chosen NLP framework. This involves feeding the encoded and embedded text data into the model, adjusting the model's parameters through an optimization algorithm (such as stochastic gradient descent), and iteratively updating the model based on the loss function's feedback.

The training process is a crucial step in building an effective language model. In this section, we will explore the steps involved in training a language model using the selected architecture and the prepared dataset.

Step-by-step instructions for the Training Process:

Step 1: Data Preparation

Before starting the training process, ensure that you have prepared your dataset by following the steps outlined in Section 2 and Section 3. The dataset should be split into training, validation, and testing sets. Also, make sure that the data is tokenized and encoded in a format suitable for the selected model architecture.

Step 2: Define Training Hyperparameters

Training a language model involves defining various hyperparameters that control the learning process. Some essential hyperparameters include:

Learning Rate: Determines the step size in the optimization process.

Batch Size: The number of data samples processed in each training iteration.

Number of Epochs: The number of times the entire dataset is used during training.

Optimizer: The optimization algorithm used for updating model parameters (e.g., Adam, SGD).

```python
learning_rate = 0.001
batch_size = 32
num_epochs = 10
optimizer = Adam(model.parameters(), lr=learning_rate)
```

Step 3: Create Data Loaders

PyTorch DataLoaders are used to efficiently load and process data during training. Create DataLoaders for the training, validation, and testing sets.

TRAINING A LANGUAGE MODEL

```python
import torch
from torch.utils.data import DataLoader, TensorDataset

# Convert your tokenized and encoded data to tensors
train_inputs = torch.tensor(train_inputs)
train_masks = torch.tensor(train_masks)
train_labels = torch.tensor(train_labels)

# Create a TensorDataset from the input data
train_dataset = TensorDataset(train_inputs, train_masks, train_labels)

# Create a DataLoader for efficient batch processing
train_dataloader = DataLoader(train_dataset, batch_size=batch_size, shuffle=True)
```

Step 4: Training Loop

The training loop is where the model learns from the data. In each epoch, the model iterates through the training data, makes predictions, calculates the loss, and updates the model's parameters based on the optimization algorithm.

```python
# Training loop
for epoch in range(num_epochs):
    model.train()
    total_loss = 0

    for batch in train_dataloader:
        inputs, masks, labels = batch
        optimizer.zero_grad()

        # Forward pass
        outputs = model(inputs, attention_mask=masks)
        loss = criterion(outputs.logits, labels)

        # Backward pass and optimization
        loss.backward()
        optimizer.step()

        total_loss += loss.item()

    # Calculate average loss for the epoch
    average_loss = total_loss / len(train_dataloader)
    print(f"Epoch {epoch+1}/{num_epochs}, Loss: {average_loss}")
```

Step 5: Validation and Early Stopping

After each epoch, it's essential to validate the model's performance on a separate validation set. Validation helps in detecting overfitting and allows you to determine the optimal number of training epochs. Implement early stopping to prevent unnecessary training and save the best model based on validation performance.

```python
best_validation_loss = float('inf')

for epoch in range(num_epochs):
    # ... Training loop ...

    # Validation
    model.eval()
    with torch.no_grad():
        total_loss = 0
        for batch in validation_dataloader:
            # Validation process similar to training loop
            # ...

        # Calculate average validation loss
        average_loss = total_loss / len(validation_dataloader)

        # Check for early stopping criteria
        if average_loss < best_validation_loss:
            best_validation_loss = average_loss
            # Save the model checkpoint
            torch.save(model.state_dict(), "best_model.pt")
```

By following these steps, you can effectively train your language model. Remember to fine-tune the training hyperparameters and experiment with different configurations to achieve the best results. Additionally, monitor the training progress, track loss values, and use validation performance to make informed decisions during training.

Hyperparameter Tuning

Fine-tune the hyperparameters of the language model to optimize its performance. Hyperparameters include learning rate, batch size, dropout rate, and regularization techniques. Experimentation and validation with different settings can help you find the best combination of hyperparameters that yield optimal results.

Hyperparameter tuning is a critical step in training a language model to achieve optimal performance. In this section, we will explore the process of hyperparameter tuning, which involves selecting the best hyperparameter values to improve the model's effectiveness and generalization capabilities.

Step-by-step instructions for Hyperparameter Tuning:

Step 1: Define the Hyperparameter Search Space

Before starting hyperparameter tuning, it's essential to define the search space for each hyperparameter. The search space includes the range of possible values for each hyperparameter that you want to explore. Common hyperparameters for language models include learning rate, batch size, number of epochs, dropout rate, etc.

```python
# Define the search space for hyperparameters
learning_rate_values = [0.001, 0.01, 0.0001]
batch_size_values = [16, 32, 64]
num_epochs_values = [5, 10, 15]
dropout_values = [0.1, 0.2, 0.3]
```

Step 2: Select the Evaluation Metric

Choose an evaluation metric that will be used to measure the performance of the model with different hyperparameter configurations. Common evaluation metrics include accuracy, perplexity, F1 score, etc., depending on the task.

```python
# For example, if the task is a language classification task
evaluation_metric = 'accuracy'
```

Step 3: Grid Search or Random Search

There are two popular approaches for hyperparameter tuning: Grid Search and Random Search. Grid Search exhaustively searches the entire hyperparameter space, while Random Search randomly samples from the search space. Grid Search can be computationally expensive, especially for large search spaces, but it guarantees finding the best hyperparameter combination within the search space. On the other hand, Random Search is more efficient but may not find the optimal hyperparameter values.

In this example, we will use Grid Search:

```python
from itertools import product

# Perform Grid Search to find the best hyperparameter combination
best_evaluation_score = 0.0
best_hyperparameters = {}

for lr, bs, ne, dp in product(learning_rate_values, batch_size_values, num_epochs_values, dropout_values):
    # Create the model with the current hyperparameter values
    model = create_model(lr, bs, ne, dp)  # You need to define a function to create the model with the specified hyperparameters

    # Train the model
    train_model(model, train_dataloader, validation_dataloader, num_epochs=ne)

    # Evaluate the model on the validation set using the evaluation metric
    evaluation_score = evaluate_model(model, validation_dataloader, evaluation_metric)

    # Check if the current hyperparameter combination is better than the previous best
    if evaluation_score > best_evaluation_score:
        best_evaluation_score = evaluation_score
        best_hyperparameters = {'learning_rate': lr, 'batch_size': bs, 'num_epochs': ne, 'dropout': dp}

print("Best Hyperparameters:", best_hyperparameters)
```

Step 4: Train the Model with Best Hyperparameters

After finding the best hyperparameters, retrain the model using the entire training dataset and the best hyperparameter values.

```python
# Create the final model with the best hyperparameters
```

TRAINING A LANGUAGE MODEL

```
final_model = create_model(best_hyperparameters['learning_
rate'],
                           best_hyperparameters['batch_
size'],
                           best_hyperparameters['num_
epochs'],
                           best_hyperparameters['dropout'])

# Train the final model using the entire training dataset
train_model(final_model, full_train_dataloader, validation_
dataloader, num_epochs=best_hyperparameters['num_epochs'])
```

Hyperparameter tuning is an iterative process that involves experimenting with different hyperparameter configurations to find the best-performing model. It requires computational resources and time, but the effort is crucial for achieving high-quality language models. Additionally, you can use other advanced hyperparameter tuning techniques like Bayesian Optimization, Genetic Algorithms, or Random Search with Early Stopping to make the process more efficient.

Validation and Evaluation

Evaluate the performance of your trained language model using appropriate metrics such as perplexity or accuracy. Additionally, perform validation tests to ensure that the model is generating coherent and meaningful text in line with your novel writing objectives.

Once the language model has been trained, it is essential to evaluate its performance and ensure that it generalizes well to new data. In this section, we will cover the process of validation and evaluation of the trained language model.

Step-by-step instructions for Validation and Evaluation:

Step 1: Split the Dataset

Before training the language model, we typically split the dataset into training, validation, and test sets. The training set is used to train the model, the validation set is used to tune hyperparameters and monitor the model's performance during training, and the test set is used to evaluate the model's final performance.

```python
from sklearn.model_selection import train_test_split

# Split the dataset into training, validation, and test sets
train_texts, val_texts, train_labels, val_labels = train_test_split(texts, labels, test_size=0.2, random_state=42)
```

Step 2: Define Evaluation MetricsSelect appropriate evaluation metrics based on the specific NLP task. For example, if the task is sentiment analysis, commonly used evaluation metrics include accuracy, precision, recall, and F1 score.

```python
from sklearn.metrics import accuracy_score, classification_report

evaluation_metrics = ['accuracy', 'precision', 'recall', 'f1']
```

Step 3: Evaluation during Training

During the training process, evaluate the model's performance on the valida-

TRAINING A LANGUAGE MODEL

tion set after each epoch. This helps monitor the model's progress and potentially early-stop the training if the performance plateaus.

```python
def evaluate_model(model, dataloader, evaluation_metrics):
    model.eval()
    predictions = []
    true_labels = []

    with torch.no_grad():
        for batch in dataloader:
            input_ids = batch['input_ids'].to(device)
            attention_mask = batch['attention_mask'].to(device)
            labels = batch['labels'].to(device)

            outputs = model(input_ids, attention_mask=attention_mask)
            logits = outputs.logits

            predictions.extend(logits.argmax(dim=-1).tolist())
            true_labels.extend(labels.tolist())

    metrics = {}
    for metric in evaluation_metrics:
        if metric == 'accuracy':
            metrics[metric] = accuracy_score(true_labels, predictions)
        else:
            metrics[metric] = classification_report(true_labels, predictions)[metric]

    return metrics
```

Step 4: Final Evaluation on the Test Set

After the training is complete, evaluate the model on the test set to assess its generalization performance.

```python
# Create a test dataloader using the test set
test_dataset = CustomDataset(test_texts, test_labels, tokenizer, max_length=max_length)
test_dataloader = DataLoader(test_dataset, batch_size=batch_size, shuffle=False)

# Load the trained model (assuming it was saved after training)
model = YourModelClass.from_pretrained(model_path)

# Evaluate the model on the test set
```

```
test_metrics = evaluate_model(model, test_dataloader,
evaluation_metrics)

# Display the test metrics
print("Test Metrics:")
for metric, value in test_metrics.items():
    print(f"{metric}: {value}")
```

Step 5: Iterative Improvement

If the model's performance is not satisfactory, consider performing hyperparameter tuning, fine-tuning on different pre-trained models, or implementing additional novel writing features to improve the model's capabilities.

Validation and evaluation are crucial steps in the NLP model development process. They help ensure that the model performs well on unseen data and meets the project's requirements and objectives. By iterating through the training, hyperparameter tuning, and evaluation process, you can fine-tune the model to achieve better results for your specific writing task.

Saving the Trained Model

Once the training is complete and you're satisfied with the model's performance, save the trained weights and parameters of the language model. This allows you to load and use the model in your novel writing tool for generating text or providing suggestions to writers.

Once you have successfully trained your language model, it is crucial to save the model's weights and configuration so that you can use it later for fine-tuning, inference, or deployment. In this section, we will cover how to save the trained model using the popular Hugging Face Transformers library.

Step-by-step instructions for Saving the Trained Model:

Step 1: Install Required Libraries

Ensure that you have the Hugging Face Transformers library installed.

```bash
pip install transformers
```

Step 2: Import Required Libraries

Import the necessary libraries to save the trained model.

```python
from transformers import pipeline, AutoModelForMaskedLM, AutoTokenizer
```

Step 3: Load the Trained Model and Tokenizer

Load the trained model and its corresponding tokenizer. Replace 'model_name' with the name of the model you used for training.

```python
model_name = "model_name"  # Replace with the name of your trained model
model = AutoModelForMaskedLM.from_pretrained(model_name)
tokenizer = AutoTokenizer.from_pretrained(model_name)
```

Step 4: Save the Model

Save the trained model and tokenizer to a directory on your local machine. Replace 'save_directory' with the desired directory path.

```python
save_directory = "path/to/save/directory"model.save_pretrained(save_directory)tokenizer.save_pretrained(save_directory)
```

Step 5: Save the Config File (Optional)

If you want to save the model's configuration separately, you can do so using the following:

```python
config = model.configconfig.save_pretrained(save_directory)
```

Step 6: Load the Saved Model (Optional)

To load the saved model and tokenizer for later use, you can use the following code:

```python
loaded_model = AutoModelForMaskedLM.from_pretrained(save_directory)
loaded_tokenizer = AutoTokenizer.from_pretrained(save_directory)
```

Now, you have successfully saved your trained language model and tokenizer, making it ready for future use. You can use the loaded_model and loaded_tokenizer to perform various NLP tasks, fine-tuning, or deploy the model in your novel writing AI system.

It is essential to save the model and tokenizer after training to avoid having to retrain the model from scratch every time you need to use it. This saves time and resources, especially when dealing with large language models and extensive training processes.

Remember that training a language model for novel writing is an iterative process. You may need to experiment with different architectures, hyperparameters, and training strategies to achieve the desired outcomes. It's recommended to consult relevant literature, research papers, and existing NLP resources for guidance on training language models effectively.

5.

Fine Tuning

Fine-tune the base language model on your specific novel writing dataset to make it more aligned with your desired outcomes. This step helps the model learn the specific patterns and nuances of novel writing.

Fine-tuning is a crucial step in creating a natural language processing (NLP) AI for novel writing. It involves customizing a pre-trained language model on your specific novel writing dataset to make it more aligned with your desired outcomes. Here's a detailed explanation of the steps involved:

Selecting a Pre-trained Language Model

Start by selecting a pre-trained language model that serves as the base for your fine-tuning process. You can utilize existing models like GPT (Generative Pre-trained Transformer) or other transformer-based models that have been trained on large-scale general text corpora. These pre-trained models have learned rich representations of language and can be fine-tuned for specific tasks.

Before fine-tuning a language model for novel writing, it's essential to choose a suitable pre-trained language model as your starting point. The selection of the pre-trained model can significantly impact the performance and effectiveness of your novel writing AI. In this section, we'll discuss how to choose the right pre-trained language model for your specific task.

Step-by-step instructions for Selecting a Pre-trained Language Model:

Step 1: Identify the Task Requirements

Understand the specific requirements of your novel writing task. Consider the language generation aspects such as grammar, style, coherence, and context. Also, consider the amount of training data available and the computational resources at your disposal.

Step 2: Research Existing Pre-trained Models

Explore the existing pre-trained language models available in the Hugging Face Model Hub or other NLP libraries like TensorFlow or PyTorch. Look for models that have been trained on vast and diverse datasets, as they are likely to capture a wide range of linguistic patterns and nuances.

Step 3: Choose Model Size and Variant

Pre-trained models come in different sizes, ranging from small to large. Larger models tend to perform better but require more computational resources and memory. Choose a model size that balances performance and resource constraints.

Step 4: Consider Fine-tuning Objective

If your novel writing task requires text generation with specific constraints, you may want to look for models that have been pre-trained on similar tasks or domains. For example, if you are writing a science fiction novel, a language model pre-trained on science fiction texts may be beneficial.

Step 5: Evaluate Language Model Performance

Before selecting a model, evaluate its performance on a small subset of your novel writing task's dataset. Use metrics like perplexity, BLEU score, or custom evaluation metrics relevant to your task. This step will help you determine if the model's pre-training aligns well with your fine-tuning objective.

Step 6: Consider Computational Resources

Take into account the computational resources available for fine-tuning. Larger models may require GPUs or TPUs for efficient training. If resource constraints are significant, consider using a smaller model or exploring distillation techniques.

Step 7: Examine Model Documentation and Examples

Review the documentation and examples provided for the pre-trained language model. Look for examples of text generation or completion tasks to assess whether the model can handle novel writing requirements.

Step 8: Fine-tuning Objective and Customization

Keep in mind that you can fine-tune most pre-trained models to adapt to your specific novel writing task. Even if a model's pre-training doesn't perfectly match your task, you can fine-tune it to improve its performance for your use case.

Step 9: Save the Selected Model

Once you have selected the pre-trained language model that best fits your novel writing needs, save its name or identifier for later use in the fine-tuning process.

By carefully selecting the pre-trained language model, you set the foundation for a successful fine-tuning process and improve the chances of developing a powerful novel writing AI system.

Dataset Preparation

Prepare your novel writing dataset for fine-tuning. This involves formatting the data in a way that is compatible with the pre-trained language model. Typically, this includes organizing the text into sequences or chunks of appropriate length that the model can process.

Before fine-tuning a pre-trained language model for novel writing, it's crucial to prepare the dataset that will be used during the fine-tuning process. Dataset preparation involves organizing the data in a format suitable for training the language model. In this section, we'll outline the step-by-step instructions for dataset preparation.

Step-by-step instructions for Dataset Preparation for Fine-tuning:

Step 1: Define the Task and Dataset Scope

Identify the specific task you want the language model to perform during novel writing. Determine the scope of the dataset, including the type of writing (e.g., fiction, non-fiction, poetry), genre, and any other relevant constraints.

Step 2: Gather the Raw Text Data

Collect a diverse and representative dataset of text relevant to your novel writing task. The dataset can be sourced from various places, such as books, articles, blogs, or online writing repositories. Ensure that the data covers the intended scope and provides enough variety for the language model to learn from.

Step 3: Data Cleaning and Preprocessing

Perform text cleaning to remove any unnecessary characters, symbols, or special formatting. Convert the text to a consistent format (e.g., lowercase) to avoid case-sensitive variations. Additionally, handle any special cases or edge scenarios that may be present in the data.

Step 4: Data Splitting

Divide the dataset into three subsets: training set, validation set, and test set. The training set is used to train the language model, the validation set is used for hyperparameter tuning, and the test set is used to evaluate the model's final performance. Typically, the split is around 70-80% for training, 10-15% for validation, and 10-15% for testing.

Step 5: Tokenization and Encoding

Tokenize the text into smaller units such as words or subwords, which will be used as input to the language model during training. Encoding converts the text tokens into numerical representations that can be fed into the model. Utilize the tokenizer provided by the pre-trained language model library to ensure compatibility.

Step 6: Padding and Batch Processing

Ensure that all the sequences in the dataset have the same length by padding or truncating as needed. Group the sequences into batches to optimize training performance. Larger batch sizes can enhance training speed, but it also requires more memory.

Step 7: Save the Preprocessed Dataset

Save the preprocessed dataset in a format suitable for training the language model. Common formats include TFRecord, Parquet, or simply as a collection of tokenized text files.

Step 8: Load the Preprocessed Dataset

During fine-tuning, load the preprocessed dataset into the language model framework. Use the DataLoader module or equivalent for efficient batch processing during training.

Step 9: Monitor Training Progress

During the fine-tuning process, monitor the training progress and performance on the validation set. Adjust hyperparameters, such as learning rate and batch size, as needed to improve the model's performance.

Step 10: Evaluate on the Test Set

After fine-tuning is complete, evaluate the trained model on the test set to assess its final performance. Use relevant metrics like perplexity or BLEU score to gauge the model's language generation capabilities.

By carefully preparing the dataset for fine-tuning, you set the stage for a successful training process that will enable your language model to effectively assist with novel writing tasks.

Model Initialization

Initialize the pre-trained language model using the weights and parameters obtained from the pre-training phase. By starting with a pre-trained model, you leverage the knowledge and language understanding it has already acquired.

In the process of fine-tuning a pre-trained language model for novel writing, one crucial step is to initialize the model with the appropriate weights and parameters. This section will provide detailed step-by-step instructions on how to initialize the language model for fine-tuning.

Step-by-step instructions for Model Initialization for Fine-tuning:

Step 1: Select a Pre-trained Language Model

Choose a suitable pre-trained language model as the starting point for fine-tuning. The choice of the base model depends on the specific task and the available pre-trained models in the NLP library of your choice. Common examples include GPT-3, BERT, RoBERTa, or XLNet.

Step 2: Install the Required Libraries

Ensure that you have installed the necessary libraries and dependencies to work with the selected pre-trained model and the NLP framework you intend to use. For instance, Hugging Face's Transformers library is widely used for working with popular pre-trained models.

Step 3: Load the Pre-trained Model

Load the selected pre-trained language model using the appropriate function provided by the NLP framework. For example, if you are using Hugging Face's Transformers library, you can use the AutoModel class to load the model by specifying its name.

```python
from transformers import AutoModel

# Load the pre-trained language model
model_name = "bert-base-uncased"  # Replace with the name of your chosen model
model = AutoModel.from_pretrained(model_name)
```

Step 4: Extend the Model for Your Task

To adapt the pre-trained language model to your specific novel writing task, you need to extend it by adding a task-specific head. The head is a neural network layer that sits on top of the pre-trained model and is responsible for the specific task (e.g., language generation for novel writing). The design of the head depends on your task and the model's architecture.

For example, for language generation tasks, you can use a simple linear layer followed by a softmax activation function to predict the next word in the sequence:

```python
import torch
import torch.nn as nn

class NovelWritingHead(nn.Module):
    def __init__(self, config):
        super(NovelWritingHead, self).__init__()
        self.linear = nn.Linear(config.hidden_size, config.vocab_size)
        self.softmax = nn.Softmax(dim=-1)

    def forward(self, hidden_states):
        logits = self.linear(hidden_states)
        return self.softmax(logits)
```

Step 5: Combine the Pre-trained Model and the Task-specific Head

Merge the pre-trained model and the task-specific head into a single model that can be used for fine-tuning. In most NLP libraries, the pre-trained model and the task-specific head are combined into a single model, allowing you to easily switch between pre-training and fine-tuning modes.

```python
from transformers import BertConfig

# Load the configuration of the pre-trained model
config = BertConfig.from_pretrained(model_name)

# Initialize the task-specific head
novel_writing_head = NovelWritingHead(config)

# Combine the pre-trained model and the task-specific head
model = nn.Sequential(model, novel_writing_head)
```

Step 6: Set Fine-tuning Hyperparameters

Define the hyperparameters for fine-tuning, such as the learning rate, batch size, and the number of training epochs. These hyperparameters significantly affect the fine-tuning process and may require experimentation to find the optimal values for your specific task.

Step 7: Prepare the Data for Fine-tuning

Load the preprocessed dataset prepared in Section 5.2 and organize it into batches for training. Use DataLoader or equivalent functionality to efficiently handle batch processing.

Step 8: Fine-tuning

With the pre-trained model and the task-specific head combined, perform fine-tuning on the novel writing dataset. Use an appropriate loss function (e.g., CrossEntropyLoss for language generation) and an optimizer (e.g., Adam or SGD) to update the model's parameters during training.

Step 9: Save the Fine-tuned Model

After fine-tuning is complete, save the fine-tuned model's weights and configuration for later use in novel writing tasks.

By following these step-by-step instructions, you can successfully initialize the pre-trained language model for fine-tuning and adapt it to your specific novel writing task. Fine-tuning allows the model to learn from the novel writing dataset and generate more relevant and context-aware suggestions for creative writing.

Training Objective

Define the specific training objective for your fine-tuning task. This objective guides the model in learning the specific patterns and nuances of novel writing. For example, you might employ techniques like masked language modeling, where the model is trained to predict missing words in a sentence, or next sentence prediction, where the model predicts the next sentence given the previous one.

In the process of fine-tuning a pre-trained language model for novel writing, defining an appropriate training objective is crucial. The training objective determines the specific task the model will learn to perform during fine-tuning. This section will provide detailed step-by-step instructions on how to define the training objective for fine-tuning the language model.

Step-by-step instructions for Defining the Training Objective for Fine-tuning:

Step 1: Understand the Task Requirements

Before defining the training objective, it is essential to have a clear understanding of the novel writing task's requirements. Determine what kind of novel writing features or suggestions you want the model to generate. For example, if you want the model to suggest plausible next sentences or predict the next word in a sentence, the training objective will differ accordingly.

Step 2: Define the Target Output Format

Based on the task requirements, decide on the target output format that the model needs to generate during fine-tuning. For instance, if the task involves predicting the next word, the target output format will be the word-level tokenization of the input text. If the task involves generating entire sentences, the output format will be the sentence-level tokenization.

Step 3: Select Loss Function

The choice of the loss function depends on the nature of the task and the target output format. For language modeling tasks like predicting the next word, the CrossEntropyLoss function is commonly used. For sequence-to-sequence tasks like sentence generation, you can use the Sequence-to-Sequence (seq2seq) loss function or other appropriate loss functions like the CrossEntropyLoss for each token in the generated sequence.

Step 4: Preprocess the Dataset

Preprocess the novel writing dataset prepared in Section 5.2 to match the target output format and the required input format for the pre-trained language model. Convert the text data into numerical representations using tokenization and encoding, ensuring that the target outputs are aligned with the corresponding input sequences.

Step 5: Prepare Data Loaders

Create data loaders to efficiently handle batch processing during fine-tuning. Data loaders help in loading and batching the preprocessed dataset, enabling smoother training on the GPU.

Step 6: Define the Fine-tuning Process

During the fine-tuning process, the model learns to generate novel writing features or suggestions based on the given input. Initialize the model with the pre-trained weights and fine-tune it using the novel writing dataset and the defined training objective.

```python
import torch
import torch.nn as nn
import torch.optim as optim

# Initialize the model with pre-trained weights (from Section 5.3)
model = nn.Sequential(model, novel_writing_head)

# Define the loss function and optimizer
criterion = nn.CrossEntropyLoss()
optimizer = optim.Adam(model.parameters(), lr=learning_rate)
```

Step 7: Train the Model

Loop over the preprocessed dataset using the data loaders and train the model using backpropagation. During each iteration, calculate the loss between the model's predictions and the ground truth target outputs. Use the optimizer to update the model's weights and minimize the loss.

```python
num_epochs = 10  # Define the number of training epochs
device = torch.device("cuda" if torch.cuda.is_available() else "cpu")
model.to(device)

for epoch in range(num_epochs):
    model.train()  # Set the model to training mode
    running_loss = 0.0

    for inputs, targets in data_loader:
```

```
            inputs, targets = inputs.to(device), targets.
to(device)

            # Zero the parameter gradients
            optimizer.zero_grad()

            # Forward pass and compute the loss
            outputs = model(inputs)
            loss = criterion(outputs, targets)

            # Backpropagation and optimization
            loss.backward()
            optimizer.step()

            running_loss += loss.item()

        # Print average loss for the epoch
        print(f"Epoch {epoch + 1}/{num_epochs}, Loss: {running_
loss / len(data_loader)}")
```

Step 8: Validation and Evaluation

After training, use a validation dataset to evaluate the model's performance on unseen data. Calculate metrics such as perplexity, accuracy, or any other relevant evaluation metric to assess the model's effectiveness in generating novel writing features.

Step 9: Save the Fine-tuned Model

Save the fine-tuned model's weights and configuration for later use in novel writing tasks.

By following these step-by-step instructions, you can successfully define the training objective for fine-tuning the pre-trained language model to generate novel writing features. The fine-tuned model will be capable of generating context-aware and creative suggestions to aid writers in their creative process.

Fine-tuning Process

Train the language model on your novel writing dataset using techniques such as backpropagation and gradient descent. During the training process, the model's weights and parameters are updated to minimize the difference between the model's predicted output and the target output. Fine-tuning allows the model to adapt to the specific writing style, vocabulary, and context of your novel dataset.

The fine-tuning process involves training a pre-trained language model on a specific dataset related to the novel writing task. This section will provide detailed step-by-step instructions on how to perform the fine-tuning process to adapt the pre-trained language model for novel writing features.

Step-by-step instructions for the Fine-tuning Process:

Step 1: Selecting a Pre-trained Language Model

Before starting the fine-tuning process, choose a suitable pre-trained language model that aligns with your novel writing task's requirements. Models like GPT-3, BERT, or OpenAI's GPT-2 are commonly used as base models for fine-tuning.

Step 2: Dataset Preparation

Prepare the dataset specifically for the novel writing task. The dataset should include text samples related to the writing features you want the model to generate, such as writing styles, character development, or plot analysis. Organize the data into appropriate formats, ensuring it is representative and diverse.

Step 3: Model Initialization

Load the selected pre-trained language model and initialize it for fine-tuning. In most cases, the base model is already pre-trained on a large corpus of text, which serves as a valuable starting point for your novel writing task.

```python
from transformers import GPT2Tokenizer, GPT2LMHeadModel

# Load pre-trained GPT-2 model and tokenizer
model_name = "gpt2"
tokenizer = GPT2Tokenizer.from_pretrained(model_name)
model = GPT2LMHeadModel.from_pretrained(model_name)
```

Step 4: Define Fine-tuning Parameters

Specify the fine-tuning parameters, including the number of epochs, learning rate, batch size, and any other hyperparameters. Fine-tuning typically requires fewer epochs than pre-training, as it builds on the knowledge already present in the base model.

```python
# Fine-tuning hyperparameters
num_epochs = 3
learning_rate = 2e-5
batch_size = 32
```

Step 5: Prepare Data Loaders

Create data loaders to efficiently handle batch processing during fine-tuning. Tokenize the input text and create data loaders that will provide batches of input sequences to the model during training.

```python
import torch
from torch.utils.data import DataLoader, Dataset

class NovelWritingDataset(Dataset):
    def __init__(self, texts, tokenizer, max_length):
        self.texts = texts
        self.tokenizer = tokenizer
        self.max_length = max_length

    def __len__(self):
        return len(self.texts)

    def __getitem__(self, idx):
        text = self.texts[idx]
        input_ids = self.tokenizer.encode(text, add_special_tokens=True, max_length=self.max_length, truncation=True)
        return torch.tensor(input_ids, dtype=torch.long)

# Assuming 'novel_texts' is a list of texts in your dataset
novel_dataset = NovelWritingDataset(novel_texts, tokenizer, max_length=512)
data_loader = DataLoader(novel_dataset, batch_size=batch_size, shuffle=True)
```

Step 6: Fine-tuning the Model

Start the fine-tuning process by iterating through the dataset and training the model using backpropagation.

```python
```

FINE TUNING

```python
device = torch.device("cuda" if torch.cuda.is_available() 
else "cpu")
model.to(device)

optimizer = torch.optim.AdamW(model.parameters(), 
lr=learning_rate)

# Fine-tuning loop
for epoch in range(num_epochs):
    model.train()  # Set the model to training mode
    total_loss = 0.0
    
    for batch in data_loader:
        batch = batch.to(device)
        optimizer.zero_grad()
        
        outputs = model(batch, labels=batch)
        loss = outputs.loss
        loss.backward()
        
        optimizer.step()
        total_loss += loss.item()
    
    # Print average loss for the epoch
    print(f"Epoch {epoch + 1}/{num_epochs}, Loss: {total_loss / len(data_loader)}")
```

Step 7: Save the Fine-tuned Model

After fine-tuning, save the fine-tuned model for later use in generating novel writing features.

```python
# Save the fine-tuned model
output_dir = "./fine_tuned_model"
model.save_pretrained(output_dir)
tokenizer.save_pretrained(output_dir)
```

By following these step-by-step instructions, you can successfully perform the fine-tuning process on a pre-trained language model to adapt it for novel writing features. The fine-tuned model will be able to generate context-aware and creative suggestions, aiding writers in their creative process.

Hyperparameter Optimization

Fine-tuning involves tuning various hyperparameters to achieve optimal performance. These hyperparameters include learning rate, batch size, regularization techniques, and others. Experimentation and validation are necessary to find the best combination of hyperparameters that yield desirable results.

Hyperparameter optimization is a crucial step in fine-tuning a language model to achieve the best performance for the novel writing task. In this section, we will explore how to optimize the hyperparameters of the fine-tuned model to improve its effectiveness in generating novel writing features.

Step-by-step instructions for Hyperparameter Optimization:

Step 1: Define the Hyperparameter Search Space

Determine the hyperparameters that can be tuned to improve the model's performance. Common hyperparameters to optimize include the learning rate, batch size, number of training epochs, and dropout rate. Define a search space for each hyperparameter, specifying the possible values or ranges.

```python
from hyperopt import hp
# Define the hyperparameter search space
space = {
    'learning_rate': hp.choice('learning_rate', [1e-5, 2e-5, 3e-5, 5e-5]),
    'batch_size': hp.choice('batch_size', [16, 32, 64]),
    'num_epochs': hp.choice('num_epochs', [3, 5, 10]),
    'dropout_rate': hp.uniform('dropout_rate', 0.1, 0.5),
}
```

Step 2: Define the Objective Function

Create an objective function that takes the hyperparameters as input, performs the fine-tuning process, and returns a metric that represents the model's performance. This metric could be the validation loss or any other relevant evaluation metric for the novel writing task.

```python
def objective(params):
    learning_rate = params['learning_rate']
    batch_size = params['batch_size']
    num_epochs = params['num_epochs']
    dropout_rate = params['dropout_rate']

    # Fine-tuning code (assuming you have already defined
```

FINE TUNING

```
'model', 'data_loader', and 'optimizer')
    for epoch in range(num_epochs):
        model.train()   # Set the model to training mode
        total_loss = 0.0

        for batch in data_loader:
            batch = batch.to(device)
            optimizer.zero_grad()

            outputs = model(batch, labels=batch)
            loss = outputs.loss
            loss.backward()

            optimizer.step()
            total_loss += loss.item()

        # Print average loss for the epoch
        print(f"Epoch {epoch + 1}/{num_epochs}, Loss:
{total_loss / len(data_loader)}")

    # Evaluation code (assuming you have validation data and
evaluation metric)
    # val_loss = ... (evaluate on validation data)

    return val_loss
```

Step 3: Perform Hyperparameter Optimization

Use a hyperparameter optimization library like Hyperopt, Optuna, or GridSearchCV to search for the best hyperparameters. These libraries use optimization algorithms to explore the search space and find the hyperparameters that minimize the objective function.

Here's an example using Hyperopt:

```python
from hyperopt import fmin, tpe, Trials

# Define the number of optimization trials
max_evals = 20

trials = Trials()
best_params = fmin(fn=objective, space=space, algo=tpe.suggest, max_evals=max_evals, trials=trials)

print("Best Hyperparameters:")
print(best_params)
```

Step 4: Fine-tune the Model with Best Hyperparameters

After finding the best hyperparameters, fine-tune the language model using those hyperparameters to obtain the optimized model.

```python
# Access the best hyperparameters from the 'best_params'
dictionary
best_learning_rate = [1e-5, 2e-5, 3e-5, 5e-5][best_
params['learning_rate']]
best_batch_size = [16, 32, 64][best_params['batch_size']]
best_num_epochs = [3, 5, 10][best_params['num_epochs']]
best_dropout_rate = best_params['dropout_rate']

# Fine-tune the model with the best hyperparameters
# ... (code to fine-tune the model with the best
hyperparameters)
```

By following these step-by-step instructions, you can effectively optimize the hyperparameters of your fine-tuned language model, leading to better performance in generating novel writing features. Hyperparameter optimization allows you to fine-tune the model for specific tasks and datasets, resulting in a more powerful and tailored AI writing assistant.

FINE TUNING

Validation and Evaluation

Evaluate the performance of the fine-tuned model on a separate validation dataset. Calculate metrics such as accuracy, perplexity, or F1 score to assess the model's performance. This evaluation helps you determine if further fine-tuning or adjustments are necessary.

Validation and evaluation are essential steps in the fine-tuning process of a language model for novel writing. In this section, we will explore how to validate the model's performance and evaluate its effectiveness in generating novel writing features.

Step-by-step instructions for Validation and Evaluation:

Step 1: Prepare Validation Dataset

Create a separate validation dataset from the original dataset used for fine-tuning. The validation dataset should be representative of the novel writing task and contain examples not seen during training.

```python
# Assuming you have a dataset and 'train_ratio' is the proportion of data used for training
from sklearn.model_selection import train_test_split

# Split the dataset into training and validation sets
train_data, val_data = train_test_split(dataset, test_size=1 - train_ratio, random_state=42)
```

Step 2: Define Evaluation Metrics

Determine the evaluation metrics suitable for the novel writing task. Common metrics include perplexity, BLEU score, or other domain-specific metrics for evaluating writing quality.

```python
# Assuming you have a function to calculate perplexity and BLEU score
def calculate_perplexity(model, data_loader):
    # Calculate perplexity for the language model on the validation set
    # ...

def calculate_bleu_score(model, validation_data, reference_data):
    # Calculate BLEU score for the generated text using reference data
    # ...
```

131

Step 3: Validate the Model

During the fine-tuning process, periodically validate the model on the validation dataset to monitor its performance. This helps in early stopping if the model is overfitting or not showing improvement.

```python
# Define the validation data loader
val_data_loader = DataLoader(val_data, batch_size=batch_size, shuffle=False)

# Validation loop
best_validation_score = float('inf')  # Initialize with a large value
for epoch in range(num_epochs):
    model.train()  # Set the model to training mode

    for batch in train_data_loader:
        # Fine-tuning code...

    # Validation after each epoch
    model.eval()  # Set the model to evaluation mode
    val_perplexity = calculate_perplexity(model, val_data_loader)
    val_bleu_score = calculate_bleu_score(model, val_data, reference_data)

    # Print validation metrics
    print(f"Epoch {epoch + 1}/{num_epochs}, Validation Perplexity: {val_perplexity}, Validation BLEU Score: {val_bleu_score}")

    # Early stopping: Save the model if validation score improves
    if val_perplexity < best_validation_score:
        best_validation_score = val_perplexity
        torch.save(model.state_dict(), 'best_model.pt')
```

Step 4: Evaluate the Fine-Tuned Model

After the fine-tuning process is complete, evaluate the model's performance on a separate test dataset, which should be different from both the training and validation datasets.

```python
# Assuming you have a test dataset
test_data_loader = DataLoader(test_data, batch_size=batch_size, shuffle=False)

# Load the best model from early stopping
model.load_state_dict(torch.load('best_model.pt'))
```

```
# Evaluate the model on the test dataset
test_perplexity = calculate_perplexity(model, test_data_
loader)
test_bleu_score = calculate_bleu_score(model, test_data,
reference_data)

print(f"Test Perplexity: {test_perplexity}, Test BLEU Score:
{test_bleu_score}")
```

By following these step-by-step instructions, you can effectively validate and evaluate the fine-tuned language model's performance for generating novel writing features. The evaluation metrics provide valuable insights into the model's effectiveness, helping you make informed decisions during the fine-tuning and iterative development process.

Iteration and Refinement

Based on the evaluation results, iterate and refine your fine-tuning process. You can experiment with different training strategies, hyperparameter settings, or even try different pre-trained models to improve the model's performance on novel writing tasks.

Iteration and refinement are crucial aspects of the fine-tuning process for a language model when crafting novel writing AI. In this section, we will explore how to iteratively fine-tune the model and refine the features to achieve better performance and writing quality.

Step-by-step instructions for Iteration and Refinement:

Step 1: Analyze Validation Metrics

After the initial fine-tuning (Section 5.5 and 5.7), analyze the validation metrics such as perplexity, BLEU score, or any other relevant evaluation metric. Identify areas where the model's performance can be improved and features can be refined.

```python
# Assuming you have already completed the fine-tuning
process and have validation metrics
val_perplexity = ...
val_bleu_score = ...

# Analyze the validation metrics
print(f"Validation Perplexity: {val_perplexity}, Validation BLEU Score: {val_bleu_score}")
```

Step 2: Identify Areas for Improvement

Based on the analysis of the validation metrics, identify areas for improvement in the model's performance and novel writing features. For example, you may observe that the model struggles with certain writing styles or has difficulty generating coherent plots.

Step 3: Adjust Fine-tuning Parameters

To address the identified areas for improvement, adjust the fine-tuning parameters such as learning rate, batch size, and training duration. You may need to fine-tune the model with different hyperparameters to find the best configuration for the specific novel writing task.

```python
```

FINE TUNING

```
# Adjust hyperparameters and fine-tune the model again
learning_rate = 1e-4
batch_size = 16
num_epochs = 5

# Fine-tuning code with new hyperparameters
# ...
```

Step 4: Implement Feature Refinements

Based on the areas for improvement identified in **Step 2**, implement refinements in the novel writing features. For example, if the model's grammar checking feature is not performing well, you may need to update the grammar checking algorithm or use a more robust language model for grammar correction.

```python
# Refine novel writing features based on identified areas
for improvement
# ...
```

Step 5: Repeat Validation and Evaluation

After implementing the feature refinements and fine-tuning the model with adjusted parameters, repeat the validation and evaluation process to measure the model's improved performance.

```python
# Fine-tuning with adjusted parameters and refinements
# ...

# Repeat validation and evaluation
val_perplexity = ...
val_bleu_score = ...

print(f"Validation Perplexity (After Refinement): {val_perplexity}, Validation BLEU Score (After Refinement): {val_bleu_score}")
```

Step 6: Iteratively Improve the Model

Iterate through Steps 2 to 5 multiple times, making further adjustments and refinements to the model and its features. The iterative process helps to gradually improve the model's performance and writing quality.

```python
```

```
# Iterate through Steps 2 to 5 multiple times
# Adjust fine-tuning parameters
# Implement feature refinements
# Repeat validation and evaluation
# ...
```

By following these step-by-step instructions and iteratively fine-tuning the language model while refining novel writing features, you can enhance the AI's ability to generate high-quality novel content. Continuous improvement through iteration is essential to achieve the desired level of performance and meet the objectives of the novel writing AI system.

By fine-tuning a pre-trained language model on your specific novel writing dataset, you enable the model to capture the unique characteristics and style of your desired writing outcomes. This step helps the AI better generate coherent and contextually appropriate text, making it a valuable tool for authors and novelists.

Remember that fine-tuning requires expertise in machine learning, NLP, and computational resources. It's important to allocate sufficient time and computational power to train and fine-tune your model effectively.

6.

Implementing Novel Writing Features

Develop features and functionalities based on your defined scope. For example, you might want to incorporate grammar and style checking algorithms, character and plot analysis modules, or even a suggestion system to provide creative prompts to the writer.

Introduction to Machine Learning Algorithms

Implementing novel writing features involves developing functionalities and algorithms based on the defined scope of your NLP AI tool. These features are designed to assist writers in various aspects of novel writing, such as grammar checking, style suggestions, character development, plot analysis, and more. Here's a detailed explanation of the steps involved:

In this section, we will provide an overview of machine learning algorithms relevant to crafting novel writing AI. Understanding the basic concepts of machine learning is essential for developing effective writing features and improving the language model's performance.

Step 1: Introduction to Machine Learning

Begin by explaining the fundamental concept of machine learning. Describe how machine learning enables AI systems to learn patterns from data and make predictions or generate content without being explicitly programmed.

Step 2: Supervised Learning

Introduce the concept of supervised learning, which is commonly used for various NLP tasks. In supervised learning, the model learns from labeled data, where inputs and corresponding outputs are provided during training. This technique is useful for tasks like grammar checking and style suggestions.

Step 3: Unsupervised Learning

Discuss unsupervised learning, another category of machine learning, where the model learns from unlabeled data. Unsupervised learning is valuable for clustering similar texts or exploring patterns within the dataset.

Step 4: Reinforcement Learning

Explain reinforcement learning, which involves an agent learning from interactions with an environment to achieve a goal. While less commonly used in natural language processing, reinforcement learning could be employed for certain aspects of the writing AI, such as generating coherent plots based on feedback.

Step 5: Overview of Common Algorithms

Provide a brief overview of common machine learning algorithms used in NLP:

a) Neural Networks: Explain the basic structure and function of neural networks, which are the foundation of many advanced NLP models.

b) Recurrent Neural Networks (RNNs): Describe RNNs, suitable for sequential data like text, due to their ability to retain contextual information.

c) Long Short-Term Memory (LSTM): Introduce LSTMs, a type of RNN designed to address the vanishing gradient problem.

d) Transformer Models: Explain the transformer architecture, which has revolutionized NLP with its attention mechanism and parallel processing capabilities.

Step 6: Transfer Learning

Elaborate on the concept of transfer learning, where a model pre-trained on a large dataset can be fine-tuned on a specific task. This approach is commonly used in NLP to leverage pre-trained language models for various writing features.

Step 7: Language Model Fine-tuning

Connect the knowledge of transfer learning with the fine-tuning process discussed in Section 5.5. Emphasize how fine-tuning a pre-trained language model enables customization for novel writing tasks.

Step 8: Selecting Suitable Algorithms

Discuss the importance of selecting appropriate algorithms based on the novel writing features required and the dataset characteristics. Different tasks may benefit from different machine learning techniques.

Step 9: Coding Example (Optional)

Optionally, provide a simple coding example illustrating the implementation of a basic machine learning algorithm for a specific writing feature using a Python-based machine learning library like TensorFlow or PyTorch.

```python
# Example of a basic supervised learning algorithm for
sentiment analysis
import pandas as pd
from sklearn.model_selection import train_test_split
from sklearn.feature_extraction.text import TfidfVectorizer
from sklearn.svm import SVC
from sklearn.metrics import accuracy_score

# Sample dataset for sentiment analysis
data = pd.DataFrame({'text': ['I love this book!', 'This
movie is terrible.', 'Great product!'],
                    'label': [1, 0, 1]})  # 1 for positive
sentiment, 0 for negative
```

```
# Split the data into training and testing sets
X_train, X_test, y_train, y_test = train_test_
split(data['text'], data['label'], test_size=0.2, random_
state=42)

# Convert text data into numerical vectors using TF-IDF
vectorizer
vectorizer = TfidfVectorizer()
X_train_vec = vectorizer.fit_transform(X_train)
X_test_vec = vectorizer.transform(X_test)

# Train a Support Vector Machine (SVM) classifier
svm_classifier = SVC(kernel='linear', C=1.0)
svm_classifier.fit(X_train_vec, y_train)

# Make predictions on the test set
y_pred = svm_classifier.predict(X_test_vec)

# Calculate accuracy
accuracy = accuracy_score(y_test, y_pred)
print(f"Accuracy: {accuracy}")
```

By providing an introduction to machine learning algorithms and their relevance to novel writing AI, readers can gain a foundational understanding of the techniques used in crafting advanced NLP features. The coding example, if included, offers a practical illustration of how to implement a basic machine learning algorithm for a writing-related task.

Grammar Checking

Develop algorithms to detect and correct grammar errors in the text. This can include identifying incorrect verb conjugations, subject-verb agreement, punctuation errors, or other grammatical inconsistencies. You can utilize rule-based approaches, statistical models, or machine learning techniques to implement grammar checking functionality.

In this section, we will explore the implementation of a grammar checking feature for the novel writing AI. The goal is to develop an algorithm that can identify and suggest corrections for grammatical errors in the text. Grammar checking is an essential aspect of improving the overall quality of written content.

Step 1: Understand Grammar Rules

Begin by familiarizing yourself with common grammar rules and errors. These may include subject-verb agreement, punctuation, verb tense, word usage, and sentence structure. It's crucial to have a solid understanding of grammar concepts before attempting to implement a grammar checking algorithm.

Step 2: Collect Grammar Corpus

To train a grammar checking model, you'll need a corpus of text with labeled grammar errors and their corresponding corrections. You can use existing grammar error datasets or manually annotate a small dataset for this purpose.

Step 3: Preprocessing

Prepare the grammar corpus by performing basic text preprocessing steps, such as tokenization, lowercasing, and removing punctuation.

Step 4: Feature Extraction

Extract relevant features from the preprocessed text, such as n-grams, part-of-speech tags, and syntactic parse trees. These features will help the model identify potential grammar errors.

Step 5: Train the Grammar Checking Model

Use a machine learning algorithm, such as a decision tree, random forest, or a neural network, to train the grammar checking model. Supervised learning can be applied here, where the input is the extracted features, and the output is the binary classification of whether a sentence contains a grammar error or not.

Step 6: Implement Error Suggestion Mechanism

Develop a mechanism to suggest corrections for identified grammar errors. This can be achieved using rule-based approaches, where specific rules are applied to suggest corrections based on the type of error. Alternatively, you can use a language model to generate contextually appropriate suggestions.

Step 7: Integrate Grammar Checking into the AI

Integrate the trained grammar checking model and error suggestion mechanism into the novel writing AI system. Ensure that the grammar checking feature seamlessly works with other writing features and provides real-time feedback to users.

Step 8: Post-processing and Refinement

Perform post-processing steps to enhance the suggestions and ensure they are contextually relevant. Refine the grammar checking algorithm based on user feedback and iterative testing.

Step 9: Testing and Evaluation

Evaluate the performance of the grammar checking feature using a separate test dataset. Measure the precision, recall, and F1-score to assess the model's accuracy in detecting grammar errors and providing appropriate suggestions.

Step 10: User Interface Integration

Design a user-friendly interface for the grammar checking feature. It should allow users to review and accept or reject suggested corrections easily. The interface can also include options for turning the grammar checking on/off or customizing its behavior.

Step 11: Continuous Improvement

Keep collecting user feedback to continuously improve the grammar checking algorithm. Use this feedback to update the model, add more rules, and enhance the error suggestion mechanism.

Note: The code implementation for the entire grammar checking feature may be extensive and beyond the scope of this book. However, this section should provide a comprehensive overview of the steps involved in developing the grammar checking component of the novel writing AI. Additionally, you can utilize existing NLP libraries like spaCy, NLTK, or LanguageTool to help implement some of the grammar checking functionalities.

Style Suggestions

Build modules that provide style suggestions to enhance the quality and coherence of the writing. This can include detecting repetitive sentence structures, identifying passive voice usage, suggesting synonyms or alternative phrases, and offering advice on improving sentence flow and clarity. Style suggestions can be implemented using rule-based approaches or statistical models trained on stylistic patterns.

In this section, we will explore the implementation of a style suggestion feature for the novel writing AI. The goal is to develop an algorithm that can analyze the writing style of the user and provide suggestions to improve the overall writing style, such as enhancing clarity, coherence, and tone consistency.

Step 1: Define Style Metrics

Begin by identifying the key style metrics that you want the AI to assess. These may include readability scores, sentence length, vocabulary richness, use of passive voice, and overall tone analysis (e.g., formal, informal).

Step 2: Data Collection for Style Analysis

Gather a diverse dataset of well-written texts with varying styles to train the style analysis model. This dataset should contain texts that represent different writing styles, tones, and genres.

Step 3: Preprocessing

Clean and preprocess the text data from the dataset. Perform tokenization, lowercasing, and remove any irrelevant elements like numbers or special characters.

Step 4: Feature Extraction

Extract relevant features from the preprocessed text to quantify the identified style metrics. For example, calculate readability scores like Flesch-Kincaid or Gunning Fog Index, count sentence length, and measure vocabulary diversity.

Step 5: Train the Style Analysis Model

Use machine learning or deep learning techniques to train the style analysis model. The model should take the extracted features as input and predict the writing style characteristics.

Step 6: Style Suggestion Algorithm

Develop an algorithm that can analyze the user's writing style using the trained style analysis model. Based on the analysis, provide relevant style suggestions to improve the writing. For example, if the user's writing is too complex, suggest simplifying sentences. If the tone is inconsistent, provide tips to maintain a consistent tone throughout the text.

Step 7: Integration with the Writing Interface

Integrate the style suggestion algorithm with the novel writing AI's user interface. Ensure that style suggestions are presented to the user in a clear and helpful manner, allowing them to easily implement the suggested changes.

Step 8: Contextual Suggestions

Consider the context of the user's writing and provide style suggestions that are contextually appropriate. For instance, the suggestions for a formal essay should be different from those for a creative fiction piece.

Step 9: User Customization

Allow users to customize the style analysis and suggestion settings according to their preferences. Some writers may prefer a more formal tone, while others may want a more casual style.

Step 10: Testing and Evaluation

Evaluate the performance of the style suggestion feature using a test dataset with varying writing styles. Measure the effectiveness of the suggestions and gather user feedback for further improvements.

Step 11: Continuous Improvement

Continuously update and refine the style suggestion algorithm based on user feedback and iterative testing. The goal is to provide personalized and contextually relevant style recommendations to enhance the user's writing experience.

Note: The implementation of a style suggestion feature may require a combination of machine learning algorithms and linguistic rule-based approaches. Additionally, utilizing NLP libraries like spaCy or NLTK can be helpful for some of the style analysis and suggestion tasks. The full code implementation for this feature may be extensive, but this section provides a comprehensive overview of the steps involved in developing the style suggestion component of the novel writing AI.

Character Development

Create features to assist with character development in novels. This can involve providing insights and recommendations on character traits, personality development, relationships, or character arcs. Develop algorithms that analyze character descriptions, actions, and dialogue to provide feedback and suggestions for consistent and engaging character development.

In this section, we will explore the implementation of a character development feature for the novel writing AI. The goal is to create a system that can help writers develop compelling and well-rounded characters for their stories.

Step 1: Define Character Attributes

Begin by defining the key attributes that make up a character, such as name, age, gender, personality traits, background, goals, motivations, and conflicts. Decide which attributes you want the AI to assist in generating or expanding upon.

Step 2: Data Collection (Optional)

If you want the AI to suggest character attributes based on real-world data or existing fictional characters, collect a dataset of well-developed characters from books or movies.

Step 3: Preprocessing (Optional)

If you have collected data, preprocess it by cleaning and organizing the character attributes. Ensure that the data is in a suitable format for training the AI model.

Step 4: Character Attribute Generation Model

Decide on the approach for character attribute generation. You can use rule-based systems, machine learning techniques, or a combination of both. If using machine learning, create a training dataset with example characters and their corresponding attributes.

Step 5: Train the Character Attribute Generation Model (Optional)

If you have chosen a machine learning approach, train the model using the prepared training dataset. Use techniques like natural language processing (NLP) to generate character attributes based on the input.

Step 6: User Input for Character Creation

Design the user interface to collect input from the writer about the type of character they want to create. This can include specifying certain traits, goals, or conflicts that the character should possess.

Step 7: Character Attribute Suggestions

Utilize the character attribute generation model to provide suggestions based on the user's input. The AI can suggest names, personality traits, and background information that align with the specified characteristics.

Step 8: Interactive Feedback

Allow the user to interact with the AI system, providing feedback on the suggested character attributes. This feedback loop can help the AI understand the user's preferences and refine subsequent suggestions.

Step 9: Character Background Stories (Optional)

If desired, consider adding a storytelling component to the character development feature. Generate background stories for the characters based on their attributes, making them more engaging and believable.

Step 10: Multiple Character Development

Allow the writer to create and develop multiple characters for their story. Ensure that the AI can keep track of each character's attributes separately.

Step 11: Integration with Writing Interface

Integrate the character development feature seamlessly into the novel writing AI's user interface. Allow the writer to access and modify character attributes while writing their story.

Step 12: Testing and Iteration

Thoroughly test the character development feature using various scenarios and user inputs. Gather feedback from writers and use it to make iterative improvements to the AI system.

Note: The character development feature can be as simple or sophisticated as desired, depending on the resources and data available. It can range from rule-based systems that generate character names and traits to more complex machine learning models that analyze existing characters' data to provide suggestions. The final implementation may involve a mix of methods to achieve the best results. Additionally, consider implementing data privacy measures if collecting and storing user-generated character information.

Plot Analysis

Implement functionalities for analyzing and improving the plot structure of the novel. This can include identifying plot holes, pacing issues, or inconsistencies in the storyline. Develop algorithms to analyze plot elements, character motivations, conflicts, and resolutions, and provide suggestions for plot development and improvement.

In this section, we will explore the implementation of a plot analysis feature for the novel writing AI. The goal is to develop an AI system that can analyze and provide insights into the plot of a story, helping writers identify strengths and weaknesses in their narratives.

Step 1: Define Plot Analysis Metrics

Decide on the plot analysis metrics you want the AI to evaluate. This can include elements like story structure, pacing, plot twists, character arcs, conflicts, and resolution.

Step 2: Data Collection (Optional)

If you want the AI to provide plot analysis based on existing stories, collect a dataset of well-structured narratives from books or movies.

Step 3: Preprocessing (Optional)

If you have collected data, preprocess it by cleaning and organizing the plot information. Ensure that the data is in a suitable format for training the AI model.

Step 4: Plot Analysis Model

Choose the approach for plot analysis. You can use rule-based systems, machine learning techniques, or a combination of both. If using machine learning, create a training dataset with example plots and their corresponding analysis metrics.

Step 5: Train the Plot Analysis Model (Optional)

If you have chosen a machine learning approach, train the model using the prepared training dataset. Utilize techniques like natural language processing (NLP) to analyze and evaluate plot elements.

Step 6: User Input for Plot Analysis

Design the user interface to allow writers to input their story or plot for analysis. This can be in the form of text or structured data representing the plot.

Step 7: Plot Analysis Suggestions

Utilize the plot analysis model to provide insights and suggestions based on the user's input. The AI can highlight areas where the plot might be strong or weak, offer suggestions for improving pacing, character development, or resolving conflicts.

Step 8: Interactive Feedback

Allow the user to interact with the AI system, providing feedback on the plot analysis. This feedback loop can help the AI understand the writer's intentions and preferences, improving subsequent analysis results.

Step 9: Comparative Analysis (Optional)

If possible, enable the AI to perform comparative plot analysis against existing well-known stories in the same genre. This can provide writers with valuable insights and benchmarks for their own work.

Step 10: Plot Analysis Reports

Generate comprehensive plot analysis reports for the writers, summarizing the strengths and weaknesses of their plot. Provide actionable suggestions for improvement.

Step 11: Integration with Writing Interface

Integrate the plot analysis feature seamlessly into the novel writing AI's user interface. Allow the writer to access and review the plot analysis while working on their story.

Step 12: Testing and Iteration

Thoroughly test the plot analysis feature using various plot structures and scenarios. Gather feedback from writers and use it to make iterative improvements to the AI system.

Note: The plot analysis feature can be tailored to the specific needs of the writer and the complexity of the AI system. It can range from simple rule-based systems that check for certain plot elements to more advanced machine learning models that provide in-depth analysis and suggestions. The final implementation may involve a mix of methods to achieve the best results. Additionally, consider implementing data privacy measures if collecting and storing user-generated plot information.

Suggestion System

Build a suggestion system that offers creative prompts and ideas to inspire writers. This can include generating prompts for plot twists, character introductions, dialogues, or settings. Implement techniques such as language models, rule-based generation, or retrieval-based methods to provide relevant and engaging suggestions to the writer.

In this section, we will explore the implementation of a suggestion system for the novel writing AI. The goal is to develop an AI system that can provide real-time suggestions and recommendations to writers as they work on their stories, helping them enhance their writing style and creativity.

Step 1: Define Suggestion Categories

Identify the types of suggestions the AI will provide. This can include grammar and spelling corrections, sentence structure improvements, vocabulary enrichment, and creative writing prompts.

Step 2: Data Collection (Optional)

If the suggestion system relies on language models and large corpora, collect a diverse and extensive dataset of written texts, including novels, articles, and essays.

Step 3: Preprocessing (Optional)

If you have collected data, preprocess it by cleaning, tokenizing, and formatting the text. Prepare the dataset for training or fine-tuning the language model.

Step 4: Language Model Selection

Choose a pre-trained language model suitable for generating creative and coherent text. Options include GPT-3, BERT, or other state-of-the-art NLP models.

Step 5: Fine-tuning the Language Model (Optional)

If the chosen language model requires fine-tuning for specific writing styles or genres, prepare a dataset of text samples that represent the desired writing style. Fine-tune the model on this dataset.

Step 6: User Input and Real-time Feedback

Design the user interface to allow writers to input their text as they write. Set up a real-time feedback system to continuously process the text and provide suggestions.

Step 7: Suggestion Generation

IMPLEMENTING NOVEL WRITING FEATURES

Implement the AI system to generate suggestions based on the user's input. Use the language model to predict and complete sentences, correct grammar mistakes, and provide relevant vocabulary recommendations.

Step 8: Feedback Presentation

Display the suggestions to the user in a user-friendly format within the writing interface. Ensure that the suggestions are presented contextually and are easily distinguishable from the original text.

Step 9: User Customization

Allow users to customize the level and types of suggestions they receive. Some writers may prefer minimal interference, while others may want more comprehensive suggestions.

Step 10: Model Confidence and Safety

Incorporate mechanisms to measure the confidence of the language model's suggestions and ensure that inappropriate or harmful suggestions are filtered out.

Step 11: Continuous Learning

Enable the AI system to learn from user interactions and improve its suggestion accuracy over time. Implement techniques like reinforcement learning or online learning for continuous improvement.

Step 12: Integration with Writing Interface

Integrate the suggestion system seamlessly into the novel writing AI's user interface. Allow the writer to enable or disable the suggestions as desired.

Step 13: Testing and Iteration

Thoroughly test the suggestion system with various writing scenarios and genres. Gather feedback from writers and iterate on the AI system to enhance its accuracy and usefulness.

Note: The suggestion system can significantly enhance a writer's creativity and productivity by providing real-time feedback and inspiration. However, it's essential to balance the system's suggestions not to stifle the writer's unique voice and style. Continuous user feedback and customization options will help strike the right balance. Additionally, consider ethical implications, such as user data privacy and AI bias, throughout the implementation process.

Real-time Feedback

Develop mechanisms to provide real-time feedback to writers as they write. This can include highlighting potential issues, suggesting improvements, or indicating areas where the writing can be enhanced. Real-time feedback can help writers iterate and refine their work as they progress, improving the overall quality of their writing.

In this section, we will discuss the implementation of real-time feedback in the novel writing AI. Real-time feedback provides writers with immediate responses and suggestions as they write, enabling them to refine their work as they progress.

Step 1: Set Real-time Feedback Goals

Identify the objectives of the real-time feedback system. Determine the types of feedback to provide, such as grammar corrections, style improvements, plot coherence, and character consistency.

Step 2: Select Feedback Metrics

Choose appropriate metrics for evaluating the quality of the writing. For example, readability scores, grammar error counts, plot consistency, and other relevant metrics can be used.

Step 3: Integrate Language Model

Integrate the selected pre-trained language model into the writing interface. This model will be responsible for generating real-time feedback based on the writer's input.

Step 4: Text Monitoring

Set up a mechanism to monitor the text input in real-time. As the writer types, continuously capture the text and analyze it for potential feedback.

Step 5: Feedback Generation

Utilize the language model to generate feedback based on the monitored text. Use NLP techniques to identify grammar mistakes, style inconsistencies, and other writing issues.

Step 6: Provide Real-time Suggestions

Display the generated feedback to the writer within the user interface. Suggestions can be presented as underlined text, pop-up notifications, or side-panel messages.

Step 7: Feedback Granularity

Allow the writer to customize the level of feedback granularity they wish to receive. Some writers may prefer detailed feedback on grammar, while others may want broader suggestions on style and plot.

Step 8: Contextual Feedback

Ensure that the feedback provided takes into account the context of the writer's work. Avoid generic suggestions that may not be relevant to the specific content being written.

Step 9: Real-time Collaboration (Optional)

If multiple writers are collaborating on a project, consider enabling real-time feedback sharing between them. This can facilitate collaboration and communication during the writing process.

Step 10: Feedback Safety and Privacy

Implement measures to ensure the privacy and safety of the writer's content. Avoid storing sensitive information and provide options for writers to disable feedback sharing if desired.

Step 11: Continuous Learning

Enable the real-time feedback system to learn from user interactions. Use reinforcement learning or other techniques to improve the quality and relevance of the feedback over time.

Step 12: User Interface Enhancement

Collect feedback from writers about the usability of the real-time feedback system and iteratively improve the user interface to enhance the writing experience.

Step 13: Testing and Iteration

Thoroughly test the real-time feedback system with various writing scenarios and gather feedback from writers. Iterate on the system to improve its accuracy and effectiveness.

Note: Real-time feedback is a valuable feature that can significantly aid writers in improving their writing skills. However, it is crucial to strike a balance between providing helpful feedback and not overwhelming the writer with constant suggestions. Customization options and continuous learning will help tailor the feedback to each writer's preferences and style. Additionally, prioritize the privacy and security of the writer's content throughout the implementation process.

Integration of Features

Integrate the developed features into a cohesive system. Ensure smooth interaction and interoperability between different functionalities. Design an architecture that allows the features to work seamlessly together, providing a comprehensive and user-friendly writing experience.

In this section, we will explore the process of integrating the novel writing features developed in the previous sections into a cohesive and user-friendly AI writing tool. Integration is a crucial step in crafting a powerful and seamless experience for writers.

Step 1: Review Developed Features

Before integration, review all the novel writing features that have been developed, including grammar checking, style suggestions, character development, plot analysis, suggestion system, and real-time feedback. Ensure that each feature has been thoroughly tested and meets the defined requirements.

Step 2: User Interface Design

Design the user interface (UI) to accommodate the various writing features. The UI should be intuitive, visually appealing, and organized to provide a smooth writing experience.

Step 3: Feature Compatibility

Ensure that the developed features are compatible with each other and do not interfere with the functionality of other features. Resolve any conflicts or overlapping functionalities.

Step 4: Modular Development

Develop each feature as a separate module that can be easily integrated into the overall AI writing tool. Use software design principles to create modular and maintainable code.

Step 5: Code Integration

Integrate the individual feature modules into the AI writing tool's main codebase. Ensure that the code is properly structured and follows best practices for readability and maintainability.

Step 6: Feature Interactions

Test the interactions between different features to verify that they work cohesively together. For example, ensure that real-time feedback does not interfere with style suggestions or plot analysis.

Step 7: User Customization Options

Provide users with options to customize the behavior and preferences of the integrated features. Allow users to enable or disable certain features, adjust feedback granularity, and personalize writing preferences.

Step 8: Error Handling and Robustness

Implement error handling and robustness measures to handle unexpected user inputs or system failures. The AI writing tool should gracefully handle errors and provide appropriate feedback to the user.

Step 9: Performance Optimization

Optimize the performance of the integrated features to ensure that the AI writing tool is responsive and efficient. Consider techniques such as caching, lazy loading, and asynchronous processing.

Step 10: Usability Testing

Conduct extensive usability testing with real writers to gather feedback on the integrated features. Use this feedback to identify areas for improvement and refine the user experience.

Step 11: Documentation and User Guides

Create comprehensive documentation and user guides to help writers understand how to use the AI writing tool and its integrated features effectively. Provide clear instructions and examples.

Step 12: Iterative Enhancement

Iteratively enhance the AI writing tool based on user feedback and changing requirements. Regularly release updates to improve the tool's performance and user experience.

Step 13: Accessibility Considerations

Ensure that the AI writing tool and its integrated features are accessible to users with disabilities. Follow accessibility guidelines to make the tool inclusive and usable for all writers.

Step 14: Version Control and Continuous Integration

Use version control systems and continuous integration pipelines to manage code changes and automate the integration process. This ensures a smooth and efficient development workflow.

By following these steps, you can successfully integrate the developed novel writing features into a powerful AI writing tool. The integration process plays a vital role in delivering a seamless and user-friendly experience that empowers writers to craft their novels more effectively.

User Customization

Consider incorporating customization options to allow writers to personalize the tool according to their preferences. This can include adjusting the sensitivity of grammar checks, customizing the style suggestions, or adapting the behavior of the suggestion system to align with the writer's unique writing style and preferences.

User customization is a critical aspect of crafting a novel AI writing tool. Allowing users to tailor the tool to their specific preferences enhances the writing experience and increases user satisfaction. In this section, we will explore how to implement user customization options in the AI writing tool.

Step 1: Identify Customization Options

Begin by identifying the key aspects of the writing process that users may want to customize. Common customization options include:

Feedback granularity: Allow users to choose the level of detail in feedback provided by the grammar checking, style suggestions, and other features.

Writing style preferences: Enable users to set their preferred writing style, such as formal or casual, and adjust the tone and voice of the AI-generated feedback.

Suggestion preferences: Let users customize the types of suggestions they receive, such as plot twists, character traits, or word choices.

Personalized dictionary: Allow users to add or remove words from a personalized dictionary to influence the AI's suggestions and language model.

Step 2: Implement User Settings

Create a user settings interface where users can modify their preferences. This interface can be a dedicated settings page within the AI writing tool or a modal window accessible from the main writing interface.

Step 3: Backend Customization Logic

Implement the backend logic to store and retrieve user preferences. Use a database or a configuration file to save user settings and ensure they persist across writing sessions.

Step 4: Feedback Loop

Integrate a feedback loop to continuously improve user customization. Provide users with the option to rate the effectiveness of the customized suggestions to fine-tune the AI model further.

Step 5: Privacy and Data Protection

Ensure that any personalized data and preferences are securely stored and that user privacy is respected. Implement data anonymization or aggregation techniques if needed.

Step 6: Sync Across Devices (Optional)

If users can access the AI writing tool from multiple devices, consider implementing synchronization of customization settings to provide a consistent experience.

Step 7: Error Handling and Validation

Include error handling and validation mechanisms in the user settings interface to handle incorrect inputs and prevent potential issues.

Step 8: Usability Testing

Conduct usability testing with a group of diverse users to gather feedback on the user customization options. Use this feedback to make improvements and refinements.

Step 9: Documentation and User Guides

Provide clear documentation and user guides explaining the available customization options and how to use them effectively.

Step 10: Accessibility Considerations

Ensure that the user customization options are accessible to all users, including those with disabilities. Follow accessibility guidelines to make the customization interface inclusive.

Step 11: Iterative Enhancement

Continuously iterate and improve the user customization options based on user feedback and evolving user needs.

By implementing user customization options, the AI writing tool can cater to the unique preferences of each writer, empowering them to create more personalized and engaging novels. Customization enhances the writing experience and encourages writers to utilize the AI tool more effectively.

Iterative Development

Continuously iterate on the implemented features based on user feedback and testing. Gather input from writers and incorporate improvements to enhance the effectiveness and usability of the tool. This iterative process ensures that the tool evolves to meet the needs and expectations of its users.

Iterative development is a crucial approach when crafting a novel AI writing tool. It involves a continuous process of refining and enhancing the tool based on user feedback, technological advancements, and evolving requirements. In this section, we will explore the steps involved in the iterative development of the AI writing tool.

Step 1: Gather User Feedback

Collect feedback from writers and users who have used the AI writing tool. This can be done through surveys, user interviews, or feedback forms integrated into the tool's user interface.

Step 2: Analyze Feedback

Thoroughly analyze the collected feedback to identify patterns, common issues, and suggestions for improvement. Categorize the feedback into different areas, such as grammar checking, style suggestions, user customization, or overall user experience.

Step 3: Prioritize Enhancements

Based on the analysis of user feedback, prioritize the enhancements and improvements that need to be implemented. Identify critical issues that require immediate attention and improvements that can enhance the user experience.

Step 4: Plan and Schedule Iterations

Create a plan and schedule for each iteration. Define the scope of each iteration and the specific enhancements to be implemented. Allocate resources and timeframes accordingly.

Step 5: Implement Enhancements

Implement the prioritized enhancements in each iteration. This may involve updating the machine learning algorithms, refining the user interface, or adding new features.

Step 6: Conduct Usability Testing

Perform usability testing on the updated version of the AI writing tool. Test it with a group of representative users to ensure that the implemented enhancements meet their needs and expectations.

Step 7: Monitor Performance

Monitor the performance of the AI writing tool after each iteration. Measure key metrics, such as response time, accuracy of grammar checking, and user satisfaction, to assess the impact of the enhancements.

Step 8: Address Issues and Bugs

Address any issues or bugs identified during usability testing or regular monitoring. Ensure that the tool functions smoothly and reliably.

Step 9: Document Changes

Maintain comprehensive documentation of the changes made in each iteration. This documentation will aid in tracking the evolution of the AI writing tool and facilitate future development.

Step 10: Seek Continuous User Feedback

Encourage users to provide continuous feedback on the tool's performance and suggest further improvements. Consider implementing a feedback mechanism within the tool for ease of communication.

Step 11: Engage in Continuous Improvement

Leverage the feedback and insights gained from users and stakeholders to drive continuous improvement. Use this information to plan subsequent iterations and prioritize future enhancements.

Step 12: Monitor Industry Trends

Stay updated with the latest trends and advancements in NLP, AI, and machine learning. Consider integrating cutting-edge techniques or models that can enhance the capabilities of the AI writing tool.

Step 13: Collaboration with Experts

Collaborate with domain experts, NLP researchers, and writers to gain valuable insights and expertise. Engaging with experts can lead to innovative solutions and improvements in the AI writing tool.

By following the iterative development approach, the AI writing tool can evolve over time, meeting the changing needs of writers and providing them with a powerful and personalized tool to craft compelling novels. Continuous improvement based on user feedback and technological advancements will ensure that the tool remains relevant and effective in the dynamic landscape of NLP for writing.

By implementing novel writing features, you enhance the capabilities of your

NLP AI tool, enabling writers to receive valuable feedback, guidance, and creative prompts throughout their writing process. The features you implement will depend on the specific requirements and scope defined for your novel writing tool. Regular updates and enhancements based on user feedback will help refine and improve the tool's effectiveness in assisting writers.

7.

User Interface

Design and build a user-friendly interface for writers to interact with your tool. Consider integrating features like text input/output, real-time suggestions, and user preferences customization.

Designing and building a user-friendly interface is a crucial step in creating a natural language processing (NLP) AI tool for novel writing. The user interface allows writers to interact with the tool effectively and enhances their experience. Here are the detailed steps involved in designing and building the user interface:

Define User Requirements

Understand the needs and preferences of the target users, which are novel writers in this case. Consider their familiarity with technology, their expectations regarding usability, and the specific tasks they need to perform with the tool. This information will guide the design process and ensure the user interface meets their requirements.

Before designing the user interface for the AI writing tool, it's essential to define the user requirements thoroughly. Understanding what users expect from the tool will help create a user-friendly and effective interface. In this section, we will explore the steps involved in defining user requirements for the AI writing tool's user interface.

Step 1: Identify User Personas

Identify and define different user personas who are likely to use the AI writing tool. User personas represent the various types of users with unique needs, goals, and characteristics. For example, there could be professional writers, aspiring authors, or students looking to improve their writing.

Step 2: Conduct User Interviews and Surveys

Conduct interviews and surveys with representatives from each user persona to gather insights into their expectations and pain points. Ask open-ended questions and prompt users to share their thoughts on the features they desire, user experience, and any challenges they face with writing.

Step 3: Analyze User Feedback

Thoroughly analyze the data collected from user interviews and surveys. Look for patterns, common requests, and pain points shared among different user personas. This analysis will be the foundation for defining user requirements.

Step 4: Prioritize User Needs

Based on the analysis, prioritize the user needs and requirements. Identify the must-have features that cater to the core needs of users and the nice-to-have features that can enhance the overall user experience.

Step 5: Define Functional Requirements

Create a list of functional requirements that describe the specific features and functionalities the AI writing tool's user interface should have. For example, real-time suggestions, grammar checking, and user customization options are potential functional requirements.

Step 6: Define Technical Requirements

Outline the technical requirements needed to implement the identified features. Consider factors such as the programming languages, frameworks, and libraries that will be used to build the user interface.

Step 7: Create User Stories

Formulate user stories to represent specific user interactions with the AI writing tool. User stories are concise descriptions of a user's goal, the actions they take, and the expected outcome. These stories help the development team understand user workflows.

Step 8: Design User Flows

Design user flows that depict how users will navigate through the AI writing tool and interact with its various features. Visualize the user journey from entering text to receiving style suggestions or grammar feedback.

Step 9: Collaborate with Designers and Developers

Work closely with user interface designers and developers to discuss and iterate on the user requirements. Collaborate to ensure that the design is feasible and aligns with the technical capabilities of the AI writing tool.

Step 10: Document User Requirements

Document all the identified user requirements, functional requirements, technical requirements, user stories, and user flows. This documentation will serve as a reference for the entire development process.

By defining user requirements in a clear and comprehensive manner, the team can build a user interface that aligns with the needs and expectations of the tool's users. Continuous communication and collaboration with designers and developers will ensure that the user interface is not only functional but also visually appealing and intuitive to use.

User Flow Design

Map out the user flow, which is the sequence of steps a user will take when interacting with the tool. Identify the key interactions and transitions between different screens or functionalities. This will help create a logical and intuitive navigation experience for the writers.

User flow design is a crucial step in crafting the user interface (UI) for the AI writing tool. It involves creating a visual representation of how users will navigate through the application and interact with its various features. In this section, we'll explore the steps involved in designing user flows for the AI writing tool's UI.

Step 1: Review User Requirements

Before starting the user flow design, review the user requirements documented in Section 7.1. Understand the core needs and goals of different user personas and how they are expected to interact with the AI writing tool.

Step 2: Identify Key User Tasks

Identify the key tasks that users will perform when using the AI writing tool. For example, key tasks may include entering text, receiving real-time suggestions, adjusting preferences, and saving or exporting the generated content.

Step 3: Create a Task Flow Diagram

Start by creating a task flow diagram that outlines the sequence of steps users will follow to complete each key task. Use simple flowchart symbols to represent each step, and connect them with arrows to show the flow of actions.

Step 4: Define User Paths

Define different user paths based on the choices users can make within the application. For example, users may have different paths for customizing preferences or accessing additional features.

Step 5: Visualize User Flows

Using wireframing or prototyping tools, create visual representations of the user flows. These visuals will provide a clearer understanding of the user journey through the AI writing tool.

Step 6: Consider UI Components

While designing the user flows, consider the UI components that will be used to facilitate user interactions. These components may include buttons, text inputs, sliders, and dropdown menus, among others.

Step 7: Account for Errors and Edge Cases

Consider error scenarios and edge cases in the user flow design. For instance, if a user enters invalid text or experiences a connection issue, the UI should handle such situations gracefully and provide informative feedback.

Step 8: Validate User Flows

Review the user flows with stakeholders, designers, and developers to ensure they align with the user requirements and capture all necessary interactions.

Step 9: Iterate and Refine

Based on feedback, iterate and refine the user flows as needed. Continuous improvement is essential to create an intuitive and user-friendly interface.

Step 10: Document User Flows

Document the finalized user flows in detail, including annotations and descriptions for each step. This documentation will serve as a valuable reference for the development team during implementation.

By designing well-structured user flows, you can ensure that the AI writing tool's user interface provides a seamless and engaging experience for users. The user flows will serve as a blueprint for the UI design and development process, guiding the team towards creating an effective and user-centric application.

Wireframing

Create wireframes, which are basic visual representations of the user interface layout. Wireframes outline the placement of different elements, such as input fields, buttons, menus, and text areas, without focusing on visual details. Use wireframes to iterate and refine the user interface structure before moving on to the visual design phase.

Wireframing is a critical step in the user interface (UI) design process. It involves creating low-fidelity visual representations of the AI writing tool's user interface. Wireframes serve as a blueprint that outlines the layout, structure, and interaction elements of the application. In this section, we'll discuss the step-by-step process of wireframing the AI writing tool.

Step 1: Gather Requirements and User Flow Diagrams

Review the user requirements documented in Section 7.1 and the user flow diagrams created in Section 7.2. Understand the key features and interactions that need to be included in the UI.

Step 2: Select a Wireframing Tool

Choose a wireframing tool that suits your needs. There are various wireframing tools available, ranging from simple online tools to more advanced design software. Some popular wireframing tools include Figma, Sketch, Adobe XD, Balsamiq, and Moqups.

Step 3: Create a Blank Canvas

Start by creating a new project or canvas in your chosen wireframing tool. This canvas will serve as the base for creating individual wireframes.

Step 4: Design the Main Layout

Begin by designing the main layout of the AI writing tool's UI. Place the key components, such as the text input/output area, navigation menu, and real-time suggestion section, in their approximate positions.

Step 5: Add Basic UI Components

Gradually add basic UI components to the wireframe, such as buttons, text inputs, checkboxes, and dropdown menus. These components should represent the essential elements that users will interact with.

Step 6: Organize the UI Elements

Arrange the UI elements logically, ensuring that the flow is intuitive for users. Consider grouping related components together and organizing them in a way that aligns with the user flow.

Step 7: Focus on Simplicity

Keep the wireframes simple and uncluttered. Avoid adding unnecessary details or high-fidelity design elements at this stage. The goal is to create a clear and easy-to-understand representation of the UI.

Step 8: Incorporate Real-time Suggestions

If the AI writing tool provides real-time suggestions, include a section in the wireframes to demonstrate how these suggestions will be displayed to the user. Consider the layout and presentation of these suggestions.

Step 9: Iterate and Get Feedback

Iterate on the wireframes based on feedback from stakeholders, designers, and potential users. Ensure that the wireframes align with the user requirements and provide a seamless user experience.

Step 10: Annotate the Wireframes

Add annotations or notes to the wireframes to provide context and additional information about specific UI elements or interactions. This will be helpful during the development phase.

Step 11: Review and Finalize

Review the wireframes one last time to ensure they accurately represent the desired UI. Make any final adjustments before finalizing the wireframes for the UI design and development process.

By wireframing the AI writing tool's user interface, you'll have a clear and well-structured plan for the UI design and development. The wireframes will serve as a visual reference for designers and developers, guiding them in creating an intuitive and user-friendly application.

Visual Design

Develop the visual design of the user interface to create an aesthetically pleasing and engaging experience for the writers. Consider factors such as color schemes, typography, icons, and overall branding elements. Ensure the visual design aligns with the goals and objectives of your NLP AI tool and creates a cohesive and enjoyable user experience.

Visual design plays a crucial role in creating an engaging and aesthetically pleasing user interface for the AI writing tool. This section will outline the step-by-step process of visual design for the tool's user interface.

Step 1: Understand the Branding and Theme

Before diving into the visual design, it's essential to understand the branding and theme of the AI writing tool. Consider the target audience, the tone of the content, and the overall look and feel you want to achieve. This information will guide the visual design process.

Step 2: Choose a Color Palette

Select a color palette that aligns with the branding and theme. Use colors that complement each other and evoke the desired emotions. It's essential to choose colors that are visually appealing and provide good contrast for easy readability.

Step 3: Select Fonts and Typography

Choose appropriate fonts for the UI. Consider using a combination of fonts for headings, subheadings, and body text. Ensure that the selected fonts are legible and consistent with the overall theme.

Step 4: Create Mockups

Using the wireframes created in Section 7.3 as a reference, create high-fidelity mockups of the user interface. Use design software like Figma, Sketch, Adobe XD, or any other tool of your choice to create the mockups.

Step 5: Design UI Components

Design individual UI components such as buttons, text input fields, dropdown menus, and other elements. Pay attention to details like button styles, hover effects, and transition animations.

Step 6: Visualize Real-time Suggestions

If the AI writing tool provides real-time suggestions, design how these suggestions will be displayed to the user. Consider using visually distinct indicators or icons to highlight suggestions.

Step 7: Design User Preferences Customization

If the AI writing tool allows users to customize preferences, design an intuitive and user-friendly customization interface. Use visual cues to indicate selected preferences and allow users to make changes easily.

Step 8: Implement Responsive Design

Ensure that the visual design accommodates various screen sizes and devices. Implement responsive design principles to make the AI writing tool accessible and usable on different platforms.

Step 9: Get Feedback and Iterate

Share the visual designs with stakeholders, designers, and potential users to gather feedback. Iterate on the designs based on the feedback received to improve the overall user experience.

Step 10: Create Design Specifications

Once the visual designs are finalized, create design specifications that outline details such as color codes, font styles, spacing, and dimensions. These specifications will be helpful for developers during the implementation phase.

Step 11: Collaborate with Development Team

Work closely with the development team to ensure the seamless implementation of the visual design. Provide any necessary assets or resources required for the development process.

By following these steps, you can create a visually appealing and user-friendly user interface for the AI writing tool. The visual design will enhance the overall user experience and make the tool more engaging and enjoyable to use.

USER INTERFACE

Text Input/Output

Provide a text input area where writers can enter their text for analysis and assistance. The output area should display the results, such as grammar and style suggestions, character and plot analysis, or any other relevant information provided by the tool. Make the text input/output areas clear and easily accessible for the writers.

In the AI writing tool, text input and output are fundamental components. This section will cover the step-by-step process of handling text input and output in the user interface.

Step 1: Design Text Input Field

The first step is to design the text input field where users can enter their writing prompts or draft content. This input field should be prominently displayed on the user interface and be easily accessible to the users.

Step 2: Implement Real-time Feedback

As users type in the text input field, the AI writing tool should provide real-time feedback, such as grammar suggestions, style recommendations, or plot analysis. This requires integrating the NLP models developed in earlier sections to process the text input and generate relevant feedback.

Step 3: Handle Text Output Display

Design a designated area or section in the user interface where the AI-generated text output will be displayed. Ensure that the text output is visually distinct from the user's input text to avoid confusion.

Step 4: Handle Real-time Suggestions

If the AI writing tool offers real-time suggestions for grammar, style, or other writing features, display these suggestions near the text output. You can use visual cues such as colored highlights or icons to indicate different types of suggestions.

Step 5: Enable User Customization

Allow users to customize the types of real-time suggestions they want to see. This can be done through user preferences customization, as mentioned in Section 7.7.

Step 6: Implement API Integration (Optional)

If the AI writing tool connects with external services or APIs, such as language translation services or sentiment analysis tools, implement the necessary API integration to enable seamless text input and output processing.

175

Step 7: Handle Special Cases

Consider special cases in text input, such as handling multiple paragraphs, special characters, or user-specific formatting preferences. Ensure that the AI writing tool can handle these cases effectively and provide appropriate feedback and suggestions.

Step 8: Implement Character Limits (Optional)

If the AI writing tool has character limits for input or output, enforce these limits in the text input and output fields. Provide clear error messages if users exceed these limits.

Step 9: Ensure Responsiveness

Make sure that the text input and output areas are responsive and adapt to different screen sizes and devices.

Step 10: User Testing and Iteration

Conduct usability testing with potential users to gather feedback on the text input and output functionality. Iterate on the design and implementation based on user feedback to enhance the user experience.

Example Code Snippet (Python - Flask Web Application):

```python
from flask import Flask, render_template, request

app = Flask(__name__)

@app.route('/', methods=['GET', 'POST'])
def home():
    if request.method == 'POST':
        # Get user input from the form
        user_input = request.form['user_input']

        # Process user input using NLP models for real-time feedback
        # (insert code for NLP processing here)

        # Generate AI output
        ai_output = "Your AI-generated text will appear here."

        return render_template('index.html', user_input=user_input, ai_output=ai_output)
    else:
        return render_template('index.html')

if __name__ == '__main__':
    app.run(debug=True)
```

USER INTERFACE

In this example, we're using Flask, a Python web framework, to create a simple web application with a text input field and text output display. The user's input is processed using NLP models (not shown in the code snippet) to provide real-time feedback. The AI-generated output is currently a placeholder but would be replaced with the actual AI-generated text in the complete implementation.

Please note that the code snippet is just an example, and the actual implementation may vary depending on the specific technology stack and requirements of the AI writing tool.

Real-time Suggestions

Implement real-time suggestions to provide writers with immediate feedback and assistance as they write. This can include highlighting potential grammatical errors, offering style suggestions, or providing prompts to enhance creativity. Ensure that the suggestions are presented in a clear and unobtrusive manner to support the writing process.

Real-time suggestions are a crucial aspect of the AI writing tool. This section will outline the steps to implement real-time suggestions for grammar checking, style suggestions, and other writing features as the user inputs their text.

Step 1: Prepare NLP Models

Ensure that the NLP models required for generating real-time suggestions are trained and ready to use. These models should be capable of processing the user's text input and providing relevant feedback.

Step 2: Define Real-time Feedback Types

Identify the types of real-time feedback you want to provide to users. This may include grammar checking, style improvements, plot analysis, or any other novel writing features you have implemented.

Step 3: Integrate NLP Models

Integrate the trained NLP models with the user interface to process the text input and generate real-time suggestions. Depending on the complexity of the models and the technology stack used, this integration may involve API calls or direct function calls to the models.

Step 4: Implement Real-time Suggestions Display

Design a visually appealing way to display real-time suggestions to users. This could be done through inline annotations, colored highlights, or pop-up suggestions, depending on the user interface design.

Step 5: Provide User Options (Optional)

Give users the option to enable or disable specific types of real-time suggestions. Some users may prefer to focus on specific aspects of their writing, and providing customization options enhances the user experience.

Step 6: Handle Performance Optimization

Real-time suggestions can put a strain on system resources, especially if the AI writing tool serves many users simultaneously. Optimize the NLP models and code implementation to ensure smooth and responsive real-time feedback.

USER INTERFACE

Step 7: Test Real-time Feedback

Conduct thorough testing to ensure that the real-time suggestions are accurate, relevant, and timely. Use a variety of test scenarios to verify the effectiveness of the suggestions for different types of writing.

Step 8: Iterate and Enhance

Based on user feedback and usability testing, iterate on the real-time suggestions implementation to improve its accuracy, user-friendliness, and overall effectiveness.

Example Code Snippet (Python - Flask Web Application):

```python
from flask import Flask, render_template, request
import nlp_models  # Assuming nlp_models contains the required NLP models for real-time suggestions

app = Flask(__name__)

@app.route('/', methods=['GET', 'POST'])
def home():
    if request.method == 'POST':
        # Get user input from the form
        user_input = request.form['user_input']

        # Process user input using NLP models for real-time suggestions
        grammar_suggestions = nlp_models.check_grammar(user_input)
        style_suggestions = nlp_models.style_suggestions(user_input)
        plot_analysis = nlp_models.analyze_plot(user_input)
        # Add more types of real-time suggestions based on your key features

        return render_template('index.html', user_input=user_input, grammar_suggestions=grammar_suggestions,
                               style_suggestions=style_suggestions, plot_analysis=plot_analysis)
    else:
        return render_template('index.html')

if __name__ == '__main__':
    app.run(debug=True)
```

In this example, we're using Flask to create a web application with a text input field. The user's input is processed using NLP models (represented by the nlp_models module) to generate real-time suggestions for grammar checking, style improvements, and plot analysis. The real-time suggestions are then displayed in the user interface (not shown in the code snippet) for the user to see.

Please note that the code snippet is a simplified example, and the actual implementation may require more complex NLP models and handling of real-time suggestions for a variety of writing features.

User Preferences Customization

Allow writers to customize the tool according to their preferences. This can include options to adjust the sensitivity of grammar checking, choose specific writing styles or genres for analysis, or personalize the tool's behavior based on their writing habits. Provide intuitive controls and settings that allow writers to tailor the tool to their specific needs.

User preferences customization allows users of the AI writing tool to tailor the system according to their individual writing preferences. This section will cover the steps to implement user preferences customization and how to incorporate it into the user interface.

Step 1: Identify Customizable Features

Determine which features of the AI writing tool can be customized by users. This could include options related to grammar checking, style suggestions, character development, plot analysis, or any other novel writing features.

Step 2: Design User Preferences Interface

Create a user-friendly interface where users can customize their preferences. This could be a settings page within the AI writing tool, accessible through the user account, or as part of the main writing interface.

Step 3: Define User Preference Options

For each customizable feature, define the options that users can choose from. For example, for grammar checking, users may prefer a more lenient or strict checking mode.

Step 4: Implement User Preferences Storage

Decide on the storage mechanism for user preferences. Depending on your application architecture, this could be stored in a database, a configuration file, or user-specific settings files.

Step 5: Integrate User Preferences with AI Writing Features

Modify the AI writing features to incorporate user preferences. For example, if users choose a specific style suggestion preference, ensure that the AI generates suggestions based on that preference.

Step 6: Provide Default Preferences

Include default preferences for users who don't customize their settings. These defaults should be carefully chosen to provide a good starting point for all users.

Step 7: Handle Preference Updates

Implement functionality to handle updates to user preferences. When users make changes to their preferences, ensure that the changes take effect immediately and apply to the writing features in real-time.

Step 8: Test User Preferences Customization

Conduct extensive testing to verify that user preferences customization works as intended and that the AI writing tool responds correctly to changes in preferences.

Step 9: Incorporate Usability Feedback

Gather feedback from users through usability testing and feedback forms. Use this feedback to refine the user preferences customization and make improvements based on user needs and expectations.

Step 10: Enhance Customization Options (Optional)

As the AI writing tool evolves and gains more features, consider expanding the customization options to cover new functionalities and user demands.

Example Code Snippet (Python - Flask Web Application):

```python
from flask import Flask, render_template, request, session

app = Flask(__name__)
app.secret_key = "your_secret_key"  # Set your secret key for session management

# Default user preferences
DEFAULT_PREFERENCES = {
    'grammar_checking': 'strict',
    'style_suggestions': 'enabled',
    'character_development': 'basic',
    # Add more preferences as needed
}

@app.route('/', methods=['GET', 'POST'])
def home():
    if request.method == 'POST':
        # Get user input from the form
        user_input = request.form['user_input']

        # Process user preferences from the session or use defaults
        user_preferences = session.get('preferences', DEFAULT_PREFERENCES)

        # Process user input using AI writing features with the given preferences
        grammar_suggestions = ai_model.check_grammar(user_input, user_preferences['grammar_checking'])
```

USER INTERFACE

```
            style_suggestions = ai_model.style_suggestions(user_
input, user_preferences['style_suggestions'])
            character_dev = ai_model.character_development(user_
input, user_preferences['character_development'])
            # Add more AI writing features based on user
preferences

            return render_template('index.html', user_
input=user_input, grammar_suggestions=grammar_suggestions,
                                style_suggestions=style_
suggestions, character_dev=character_dev)
    else:
            return render_template('index.html')

@app.route('/preferences', methods=['GET', 'POST'])
def preferences():
    if request.method == 'POST':
        # Get user preferences from the form
        user_preferences = {
            'grammar_checking': request.form.get('grammar_
checking'),
            'style_suggestions': request.form.get('style_
suggestions'),
            'character_development': request.form.
get('character_development'),
            # Add more preferences as needed
        }

        # Store user preferences in the session
        session['preferences'] = user_preferences

        return render_template('preferences.html',
preferences=user_preferences)
    else:
        # Retrieve user preferences from the session or use
defaults
        user_preferences = session.get('preferences',
DEFAULT_PREFERENCES)
        return render_template('preferences.html',
preferences=user_preferences)

if __name__ == '__main__':
    app.run(debug=True)
```

In this example, we're using Flask to create a web application with two routes: the home route (/) for the main writing interface and the preferences route (/preferences) for the user preferences customization. The user preferences are stored in the session, allowing them to persist across different pages. Users can access the preferences page to customize their settings, and the preferences will be applied to the AI writing features in real-time.

Please note that the code snippet is a simplified example, and the actual implementation may require more customization options and user interface elements to provide a comprehensive user preferences customization experience.

Usability Testing

Conduct usability testing to evaluate the effectiveness and efficiency of the user interface. Engage a group of representative writers or beta testers to perform tasks using the tool and collect feedback on their experience. Analyze the feedback to identify any usability issues, areas for improvement, or features that may need further refinement.

Usability testing is a critical phase in the development of the AI writing tool's user interface. It helps identify potential issues, gather feedback from real users, and ensure that the interface is intuitive and user-friendly. This section will cover the steps to conduct usability testing and how to incorporate the feedback into the design and development process.

Step 1: Define Usability Testing Goals

Establish clear goals and objectives for the usability testing. Determine the specific aspects of the user interface that need to be evaluated, such as ease of use, navigation, feature discoverability, and overall user satisfaction.

Step 2: Recruit Test Participants

Recruit a diverse group of test participants who represent the target user demographic. Aim to have a mix of individuals with varying levels of writing experience and familiarity with AI tools. Typically, 5-10 participants are sufficient for a usability test.

Step 3: Create Usability Test Scenarios

Develop a set of test scenarios that reflect common tasks users would perform with the AI writing tool. For example, ask participants to write a short story using the grammar checking and style suggestion features.

Step 4: Set Up the Usability Test Environment

Prepare the testing environment with the AI writing tool and any necessary hardware or software. Ensure that the tool is in a stable state and ready for testing.

Step 5: Conduct the Usability Test

One by one, guide each participant through the usability test scenarios while observing their interactions with the AI writing tool. Encourage participants to think aloud as they use the tool and take note of any issues or feedback they provide.

Step 6: Gather Feedback and Observations

Record both qualitative and quantitative data during the usability tests. Take notes on participants' comments, observations, and any areas where they encountered difficulties or confusion.

Step 7: Analyze Usability Test Results

Review the data collected from the usability tests and identify patterns or recurring issues. Categorize the feedback into critical, major, and minor usability problems.

Step 8: Address Critical and Major Issues

Prioritize the critical and major usability problems and work with the development team to address them promptly. This may involve redesigning certain features, improving the user flow, or making the interface more intuitive.

Step 9: Iterate and Improve

Make the necessary improvements based on the usability test feedback and conduct further testing to verify the effectiveness of the changes. Iteratively refine the user interface based on user feedback until the major usability issues are resolved.

Step 10: Prepare for Beta Testing

Once the major usability problems have been addressed, prepare the AI writing tool for beta testing. Invite a larger group of users to try out the tool and gather additional feedback to make final adjustments.

Step 11: Document Usability Test Findings

Create a comprehensive report summarizing the usability test findings, the changes made based on the feedback, and any ongoing usability concerns that require attention in future iterations.

Step 12: Repeat Usability Testing (As Needed)

Throughout the development process and after each major update, continue conducting usability testing to ensure the ongoing improvement of the user interface.

Example Code Snippet (Python - Usability Testing Script):

```python
def usability_test(scenarios, ai_writing_tool):
    test_results = []

    for scenario in scenarios:
        user_input = scenario['input']
        expected_output = scenario['expected_output']

        # Simulate user interactions with the AI writing
```

USER INTERFACE

```
tool
        actual_output = ai_writing_tool.process(user_input)

        # Check if the actual output matches the expected output
        success = (actual_output == expected_output)

        test_results.append({
            'scenario': scenario['name'],
            'success': success,
            'actual_output': actual_output,
            'expected_output': expected_output
        })

    return test_results

if __name__ == '__main__':
    # Sample usability test scenarios
    scenarios = [
        {
            'name': 'Grammar Checking Scenario',
            'input': 'He enjoy playing soccer.',
            'expected_output': 'He enjoys playing soccer.'
        },
        {
            'name': 'Style Suggestion Scenario',
            'input': 'The weather is good.',
            'expected_output': 'The weather is excellent.'
        },
        # Add more usability test scenarios
    ]

    # Sample AI writing tool
    class AIWritingTool:
        def process(self, user_input):
            # Simulate AI processing based on user input
            # Replace this with the actual AI processing logic
            return user_input

    ai_tool = AIWritingTool()

    # Run usability test
    results = usability_test(scenarios, ai_tool)

    # Display test results
    for result in results:
        print(f"Scenario: {result['scenario']}")
        print(f"Success: {result['success']}")
        print(f"Expected Output: {result['expected_output']}")
        print(f"Actual Output: {result['actual_output']}")
        print()
```

In this example, we have a simple usability testing script that runs a set of test scenarios against a sample AI writing tool. The usability_test function takes a list of test scenarios and the AI writing tool as input and returns the results of the tests. The test scenarios include sample user inputs and their corresponding expected outputs. The AI writing tool is a placeholder class simulating AI processing, and the actual implementation would involve a real AI model.

Please note that this example is a simplified representation of usability testing. In a real-world scenario, usability testing would involve real users interacting with the AI writing tool, and the actual implementation would be more comprehensive.

Iteration and Enhancement

Based on the feedback received from usability testing, iteratively improve and enhance the user interface. Address any identified usability issues, streamline the user flow, and incorporate user suggestions to enhance the overall user experience. Repeat the usability testing process after each iteration to validate the changes and ensure continual improvement.

Once the initial version of the user interface for the AI writing tool has been developed and usability testing has been conducted, it's time to iterate and enhance the user interface based on the feedback received from users. This section will cover the steps involved in the iteration and enhancement process.

Step 1: Analyze Usability Test Feedback

Review the results and feedback from the usability testing conducted in Section 7.8. Identify the major pain points, usability issues, and suggestions for improvement provided by the test participants.

Step 2: Prioritize Changes

Prioritize the changes and enhancements based on the severity of the usability issues and their impact on the overall user experience. Focus on addressing critical and major issues first.

Step 3: Collaborate with the Development Team

Work closely with the development team to discuss the feedback and proposed changes. Ensure that the team is aware of the user requirements and understands the objectives of the enhancements.

Step 4: Design and Implement Changes

Based on the prioritized changes, design the necessary improvements in the user interface. This may involve redesigning certain features, updating the layout, or adding new functionalities. Collaborate with the development team to implement these changes.

Step 5: Conduct Internal Testing

Before releasing the updated user interface to users, conduct internal testing to ensure that the implemented changes work as expected and do not introduce new issues.

Step 6: Update Documentation and User Guides

Update the documentation and user guides to reflect the changes and enhancements made in the user interface. Provide clear and comprehensive instructions on how to use the new features.

Step 7: Inform Users of Changes

If the AI writing tool is already in use by a user base, inform them about the upcoming changes and enhancements. Provide clear communication about the benefits of the updates and any necessary instructions for adapting to the changes.

Step 8: Release the Updated User Interface

Once the internal testing is completed and users are informed, release the updated user interface. Monitor the release closely to ensure that there are no unexpected issues and that the enhancements are positively received.

Step 9: Gather User Feedback on Enhancements

Encourage users to provide feedback on the new version of the user interface. Pay close attention to user reactions, comments, and suggestions for further improvement.

Step 10: Iterate and Repeat

Based on the feedback received from users, iterate further to make continuous improvements to the user interface. This process of iteration and enhancement should be ongoing to ensure that the AI writing tool evolves to meet user needs and preferences.

Example Code Snippet (Python - Handling User Feedback):

```python
def gather_user_feedback():
    # Function to collect user feedback through surveys, feedback forms, etc.
    feedback_results = []

    # Implement the code to gather user feedback

    return feedback_results

def process_user_feedback(feedback_results, ui_enhancements):
    for feedback in feedback_results:
        if feedback['type'] == 'issue':
            # Analyze user-reported issues and bugs
            if feedback['severity'] == 'critical':
                # Address critical issues immediately
                # Collaborate with the development team to fix critical issues

        elif feedback['type'] == 'suggestion':
            # Analyze user suggestions for UI enhancements
```

USER INTERFACE

```python
        if feedback['impact'] == 'major':
            # Prioritize major UI enhancements and
collaborate with the development team to implement them

    # Implement the code to update the user interface based
on the processed feedback

if __name__ == '__main__':
    # Assuming feedback_results is a list of feedback
received from users
    feedback_results = [
        {
            'type': 'issue',
            'severity': 'major',
            'description': 'The grammar checking feature
sometimes gives incorrect suggestions.'
        },
        {
            'type': 'suggestion',
            'impact': 'minor',
            'description': 'It would be helpful to have a
character count feature in the text editor.'
        },
        # Add more feedback entries
    ]

    # Assuming ui_enhancements is a list of proposed UI
changes based on the feedback
    ui_enhancements = [
        {
            'feature': 'Grammar Checking',
            'description': 'Improve grammar checking
accuracy.'
        },
        {
            'feature': 'Text Editor',
            'description': 'Add character count feature.'
        },
        # Add more proposed UI enhancements
    ]

    # Process user feedback and update the user interface
    process_user_feedback(feedback_results, ui_enhancements)
```

In this example, we have a simplified Python code snippet for handling user feedback and implementing UI enhancements based on the feedback. The gather_user_feedback function simulates the collection of user feedback, and the process_user_feedback function processes the feedback and updates the UI accordingly. In a real-world scenario, the feedback collection process would involve user feedback mechanisms, such as surveys or feedback forms, and the actual implementation of UI changes would be more comprehensive.

By designing and building a user-friendly interface for your NLP AI tool, you can provide writers with an intuitive and efficient platform for utilizing its features and functionalities. The user interface should seamlessly integrate with the tool's capabilities and enhance the writer's creative process while providing valuable assistance in novel writing.

8.

Testing and Iteration

Thoroughly test your tool with different novel writing scenarios and gather feedback from writers. Iterate on the features, model, and user interface based on user feedback to improve the tool's effectiveness and usability.

Testing and iteration are crucial steps in the development of your NLP AI tool for novel writing. These steps involve thoroughly testing the tool with different novel writing scenarios, gathering feedback from writers, and iterating on the features, model, and user interface to improve the tool's effectiveness and usability. Here's a detailed explanation of the steps involved:

Test Scenario Design

Define a set of test scenarios that cover various aspects of novel writing. Consider different writing styles, genres, and specific challenges that writers may encounter. Test scenarios can include grammar and style checking, character and plot analysis, suggestion system evaluation, and user interface usability testing.

In this section, we will focus on designing test scenarios for the AI writing tool. Test scenarios are specific situations or conditions under which the tool's functionality will be tested to ensure its effectiveness, accuracy, and robustness.

Step 1: Identify Test Objectives

Before designing test scenarios, it's crucial to identify the objectives of the testing phase. Determine what aspects of the AI writing tool you want to evaluate and verify. Possible objectives could include testing the accuracy of grammar checking, the relevance of style suggestions, and the effectiveness of the suggestion system.

Step 2: Define Test Cases

Based on the identified objectives, create individual test cases that represent specific scenarios. Each test case should have a clear description of the scenario, expected outcomes, and the steps required to execute the test.

Step 3: Consider Different Inputs

Design test scenarios that cover a variety of input types and styles. For grammar checking, include test cases with sentences containing common grammatical errors, complex sentence structures, and varying writing styles. For style suggestions, include test cases with different genres and writing tones.

Step 4: Cover Edge Cases

Include test scenarios that address edge cases, i.e., situations that may occur infrequently or in extreme conditions. For instance, test the AI writing tool's behavior when presented with very short or excessively long text passages.

Step 5: Handle Multilingual Support (If Applicable)

If the AI writing tool supports multiple languages, design test scenarios to cover different languages and ensure the tool performs well across various language inputs.

Step 6: Determine Success Criteria

Define clear success criteria for each test scenario. These criteria will help you determine whether the tool has passed the test successfully. Success criteria could include achieving a certain accuracy level for grammar checking or receiving a high relevance score for style suggestions.

Step 7: Prepare Test Data

Collect or generate the test data required for each test scenario. For grammar checking, create a set of sentences with predefined errors. For style suggestions, have a collection of writing samples representing different writing styles and genres.

Step 8: Implement Test Automation (Optional)

Consider implementing test automation for repetitive or time-consuming test cases. Test automation can speed up the testing process and improve accuracy. Use testing frameworks like PyTest or Selenium, depending on the nature of the testing.

Step 9: Execute Test Scenarios

Follow the steps outlined in each test case to execute the test scenarios. Record the results, including any errors or unexpected behavior encountered during the testing process.

Step 10: Analyze Results and Debug

After executing the test scenarios, analyze the results against the defined success criteria. If any test cases fail, investigate the reasons for failure and debug the AI writing tool accordingly.

Step 11: Iterate and Enhance

Based on the test results and user feedback, identify areas for improvement and iterate on the AI writing tool's features. Implement necessary enhancements and conduct additional testing as required.

Step 12: Document Test Results

Record the test results, including test case descriptions, inputs, expected outcomes, actual outcomes, and any issues encountered during testing. This documentation will be valuable for future reference and for tracking improvements over time.

TESTING AND ITERATION

Example Code Snippet (Python - PyTest):

```python
# Sample PyTest implementation for grammar checking test scenario

# Assuming you have a function `grammar_check` that performs grammar checking
def grammar_check(text):
    # Your grammar checking implementation here
    pass

def test_grammar_check():
    # Test case 1: Sentence with a common grammatical error
    sentence1 = "He don't like this book."
    assert grammar_check(sentence1) == "He doesn't like this book."

    # Test case 2: Complex sentence structure
    sentence2 = "Despite the heavy rain, Mary went out to play tennis."
    assert grammar_check(sentence2) == "Despite the heavy rain, Mary went out to play tennis."

    # Test case 3: Very short sentence
    sentence3 = "I am."
    assert grammar_check(sentence3) == "I am."

    # Test case 4: Excessively long sentence
    sentence4 = "This is a very long sentence that goes on and on and on and on and on and on and on and on and on and on."
    assert grammar_check(sentence4) == "This is a very long sentence that goes on and on and on and on and on and on and on and on and on and on."
```

In this example, we use PyTest, a popular testing framework in Python, to implement test scenarios for grammar checking. Each test case represents a specific sentence with different characteristics, and we use the assert statement to verify the expected output from the grammar_check function. Run PyTest to execute the test scenarios and ensure the grammar checking functionality works as expected.

Note: The actual implementation of the grammar checking function is not provided in this example, as it may vary depending on the specific grammar checking algorithm you choose to use. The code snippet demonstrates the test structure using PyTest.

Test Execution

Execute the defined test scenarios using the developed tool. This involves simulating realistic writing situations and evaluating the tool's performance against expected outcomes. Pay attention to the tool's response time, accuracy of suggestions, effectiveness in identifying errors or inconsistencies, and the overall user experience.

In this section, we will discuss the process of executing the test scenarios designed in Section 8.1 for the AI writing tool. Test execution involves running the test cases and observing the actual outcomes to determine whether the tool functions as expected.

Step 1: Test Environment Setup

Before starting the test execution, ensure that you have set up the test environment properly. This includes having the AI writing tool deployed in a suitable testing environment with all the necessary dependencies and resources available.

Step 2: Test Data Preparation

Ensure that the test data required for each test scenario is readily available. This may include sample text passages, writing styles, genres, and any other data relevant to the specific test cases.

Step 3: Test Case Execution

Execute each test case one by one. During the execution, carefully follow the steps outlined in each test case and input the corresponding test data.

Step 4: Observe and Record Outcomes

As the test cases are executed, observe the tool's behavior and record the actual outcomes. Compare the actual outcomes with the expected outcomes defined in the test cases.

Step 5: Defect Reporting

If any test case produces results that deviate from the expected outcomes or reveals defects in the AI writing tool, report these issues promptly. Use a defect tracking system to log and manage the reported defects.

Step 6: Regression Testing (Optional)

If defects are identified and fixed during the testing process, consider performing regression testing. Regression testing involves re-running the affected test cases and other related test scenarios to ensure that the defect fixes do not introduce new issues.

TESTING AND ITERATION

Step 7: Collect User Feedback

Gather feedback from users who participate in the user acceptance testing (UAT) phase. Their feedback can provide valuable insights into the tool's usability, user experience, and any areas that require improvement.

Step 8: Monitor Performance Metrics

During the test execution, monitor performance metrics such as response time, memory usage, and system resource consumption. Assess whether the AI writing tool meets the required performance criteria.

Step 9: Analyze Test Results

After completing the test execution, analyze the test results and compare them with the defined success criteria. Identify any discrepancies, issues, or areas for improvement.

Step 10: Collaborate with Development Team

Work closely with the development team to address the reported defects and implement necessary enhancements based on the test results and user feedback.

Step 11: Documentation

Record the test execution results, including test case execution logs, observed outcomes, defect reports, and any performance metrics. This documentation will be essential for future reference and improvement iterations.

Step 12: Prepare User Guides and Documentation

Based on the test results and final version of the AI writing tool, create comprehensive user guides and documentation. These documents should explain how to use the tool effectively and provide troubleshooting guidelines.

Example Code Snippet (Python - PyTest):

```python
# Sample PyTest implementation for test execution

# Assuming you have a function `run_ai_tool` that executes the AI writing tool
def run_ai_tool(input_text):
    # Your AI writing tool execution implementation here
    pass

def test_ai_tool():
    # Test case 1: Grammar checking test
    input_text1 = "He don't like this book."
    assert run_ai_tool(input_text1) == "He doesn't like this
```

```
book."

    # Test case 2: Style suggestions test
    input_text2 = "I'm going to the store."
    assert run_ai_tool(input_text2) == "I am going to the
store."

    # Test case 3: Character development test
    input_text3 = "John was a brave and adventurous soul."
    assert run_ai_tool(input_text3) == "John was a brave and
adventurous soul."

    # Test case 4: Real-time feedback test
    input_text4 = "This story is going great!"
    assert run_ai_tool(input_text4) == "This story is going
great!"
```

In this example, we use PyTest to execute the test scenarios for the AI writing tool. Each test case represents a specific test scenario for grammar checking, style suggestions, character development, and real-time feedback. The assert statements verify the actual outcomes of the AI writing tool against the expected results. Run PyTest to execute the test cases and ensure the AI writing tool functions correctly.

Gather User Feedback

Collect feedback from writers who have used the tool. This can be done through surveys, interviews, or user testing sessions. Encourage users to provide detailed feedback on the tool's strengths, weaknesses, and areas for improvement. Consider their suggestions for additional features or enhancements that could enhance the tool's utility.

Gathering user feedback is a crucial step in the testing and iteration process of the AI writing tool. User feedback provides valuable insights into the tool's usability, effectiveness, and user experience. In this section, we will outline the steps to effectively gather user feedback for the AI writing tool.

Step 1: Plan User Feedback Collection

Before reaching out to users, create a well-defined plan for gathering feedback. Decide on the specific aspects you want to collect feedback on, such as user satisfaction, tool performance, feature usability, and any specific areas of improvement.

Step 2: Identify User Groups

Identify different user groups who will be providing feedback. This can include writers, editors, content creators, and other potential users of the AI writing tool. Consider selecting users with diverse backgrounds and writing styles to ensure a broader range of feedback.

Step 3: Prepare Feedback Survey or Questionnaire

Create a feedback survey or questionnaire that captures the essential information you want to collect. The questions should be clear, concise, and focused on actionable insights. Include both qualitative and quantitative questions to gather detailed feedback.

Step 4: Conduct User Interviews (Optional)

In addition to surveys, consider conducting one-on-one user interviews to gain deeper insights into user experiences and pain points. User interviews allow for open-ended discussions and provide opportunities for users to express their thoughts more freely.

Step 5: Choose Feedback Collection Methods

Decide on the methods for collecting user feedback. Common methods include online surveys, email feedback requests, in-person interviews, and feedback forms integrated into the AI writing tool's user interface.

Step 6: Reach Out to Users

Contact the identified user groups and request their participation in providing feedback. Clearly explain the purpose of the feedback and assure users that their responses will remain confidential and anonymous, if applicable.

Step 7: Gather and Analyze Feedback

As users provide feedback, collect and analyze the responses systematically. Look for common patterns and themes in the feedback. Identify both positive aspects of the tool and areas that require improvement.

Step 8: Prioritize Feedback

Prioritize the feedback based on the impact it may have on the AI writing tool's usability and effectiveness. Address critical issues first and consider user suggestions for enhancing existing features or adding new ones.

Step 9: Share Feedback with the Development Team

Collaborate with the development team to share the gathered user feedback. Work together to interpret the feedback and devise appropriate action plans to address the identified issues and implement necessary improvements.

Step 10: Implement Enhancements

Based on the user feedback and collaboration with the development team, implement the necessary enhancements to the AI writing tool. This may involve bug fixes, performance optimizations, and adding new features.

Step 11: Inform Users of Updates

Keep the user groups informed about the updates and improvements made to the AI writing tool based on their feedback. Transparent communication with users shows that their input is valued and encourages further engagement.

Step 12: Continuous Feedback Collection

User feedback should be an ongoing process. Encourage continuous feedback collection to ensure that the AI writing tool remains relevant and effective in meeting users' evolving needs.

Example Feedback Survey Questions:

1. *On a scale of 1 to 5, how satisfied are you with the AI writing tool's grammar checking feature?*
2. *What specific improvements would you like to see in the style suggestions provided by the tool?*
3. *How frequently do you use the character development feature? Please share any thoughts or suggestions regarding this feature.*
4. *Does the real-time feedback system effectively help you in improving your writing? If not,*

TESTING AND ITERATION

    what could be done to enhance it?

5. *How would you rate the overall user experience of the AI writing tool?*
6. *Is there any particular feature missing that you believe would significantly benefit your writing process?*
7. *Are there any challenges or difficulties you encountered while using the tool? If yes, please explain.*
8. *What do you like most about the AI writing tool?*
9. *How likely are you to recommend this tool to a fellow writer or colleague?*
10. *Do you have any additional comments or feedback that you would like to share with us?*

Gathering feedback from actual users is essential to iteratively improve the AI writing tool and make it more valuable to its target audience. The process of user feedback collection should be conducted with empathy, transparency, and a commitment to addressing users' needs and concerns.

205

Analyze Feedback and Identify Issues

Analyze the gathered feedback to identify common patterns, issues, and areas of improvement. Look for recurring problems, usability challenges, or functionality gaps that hinder the tool's performance. Prioritize the issues based on their impact and the frequency of occurrence.

Iterative Development

Based on the identified issues and user feedback, iterate on the features, model, and user interface to address the identified problems. This may involve refining existing features, adding new functionalities, or modifying the tool's behavior based on user preferences. Aim to improve the tool's effectiveness, accuracy, and user satisfaction.

Iterative development is a crucial aspect of the testing and iteration process for the AI writing tool. It involves making incremental improvements to the tool based on user feedback and continuous testing. In this section, we will outline the steps for iterative development to enhance the AI writing tool's performance and user experience.

Step 1: Analyze User Feedback

Before proceeding with iterative development, carefully analyze the user feedback gathered during the testing phase (Section 8.4). Identify common patterns, pain points, and areas where the tool can be improved.

Step 2: Set Improvement Priorities

Based on the analysis of user feedback, set priorities for the improvements you want to make to the AI writing tool. Determine which features or aspects are most critical to address and which enhancements can be deferred to subsequent iterations.

Step 3: Define Iteration Goals

For each iteration, define clear and achievable goals. These goals should align with the user feedback and the identified priorities. Be specific about what you want to accomplish in the current iteration.

Step 4: Implement Incremental Changes

Begin the iterative development by implementing incremental changes to the AI writing tool. Focus on the improvements identified in the previous steps. Make adjustments to the existing features, fix bugs, and add new functionalities as needed.

Step 5: Test and Validate Changes

Thoroughly test the changes introduced in the current iteration. Conduct both automated testing and manual testing to ensure the tool functions correctly and that the new features or improvements have been effectively integrated.

Step 6: Gather Feedback for the Current Iteration

During the current iteration, continue to gather feedback from users who are using the updated version of the AI writing tool. Encourage users to provide feedback on the new features and improvements.

Step 7: Assess Iteration Success

At the end of the iteration, assess the success of the changes made. Evaluate whether the goals defined for the iteration have been achieved and whether the user feedback indicates positive outcomes.

Step 8: Document Changes and Feedback

Document all the changes made during the current iteration, including code modifications, bug fixes, and new feature implementations. Also, document the feedback received from users during the iteration.

Step 9: Plan the Next Iteration

Use the insights gained from the current iteration to plan the next iteration. Based on the feedback and assessment, set new improvement priorities and define iteration goals for further enhancing the tool.

Step 10: Iterate Continuously

Repeat the process of iterative development with each new iteration. Continue to gather user feedback, implement improvements, and validate changes. The AI writing tool should evolve over time to meet user needs and expectations effectively.

Step 11: Version Control and Collaboration

Use version control systems (e.g., Git) to manage the changes made during each iteration. This allows for collaboration among team members and ensures that the tool's development history is well-maintained.

Step 12: Release Updates

Periodically release updates to the AI writing tool with the accumulated improvements from multiple iterations. Inform users about the updates and encourage them to install the latest version for the best experience.

Remember that iterative development is an ongoing process, and the AI writing tool should continuously evolve and improve based on user feedback and changing requirements. A well-executed iterative development approach ensures that the tool remains relevant, efficient, and valuable to its users over time.

(Note: The code blocks and reference links mentioned in this book are not provided in this response as the implementation of an AI writing tool and its iterative development require complex programming and domain-specific knowledge. It's recommended to consult relevant machine learning and natural language processing resources and collaborate with a team of experts for the actual development of the AI writing tool.)

Testing Enhancements

Repeat the testing process with the enhanced version of the tool. Execute the test scenarios and evaluate the tool's performance to ensure that the implemented changes have effectively addressed the identified issues and improved the tool's overall performance.

Testing enhancements is a crucial step in the iterative development process for the AI writing tool. As new features and improvements are implemented, it's essential to thoroughly test them to ensure they work as expected and do not introduce any unintended issues. In this section, we will outline the steps for testing enhancements in the AI writing tool.

Step 1: Review Enhancement Specifications

Before beginning the testing process, review the specifications of the enhancements that have been implemented. Ensure that you have a clear understanding of what each enhancement is intended to achieve and how it should behave.

Step 2: Unit Testing

Perform unit testing on individual components or modules that have been enhanced. Unit testing involves testing each unit (e.g., functions, methods) in isolation to verify their correctness. Write test cases for each unit and execute them to identify and fix any bugs or issues.

Step 3: Integration Testing

Conduct integration testing to verify that the enhanced components work together as expected when integrated into the AI writing tool. Test the interactions between different modules and functionalities to ensure they are seamless and do not cause conflicts.

Step 4: Regression Testing

Perform regression testing to ensure that the new enhancements have not adversely affected existing features. Re-run previous test cases to check if the enhancements have introduced any unintended side effects or broken any existing functionalities.

Step 5: User Acceptance Testing (UAT)

Invite a group of real users or beta testers to perform user acceptance testing. Provide them with access to the AI writing tool's updated version and gather their feedback on the new features and improvements. Use their input to identify any usability issues or areas for further enhancement.

Step 6: Performance Testing

Conduct performance testing to evaluate the speed and efficiency of the AI writing tool with the new enhancements. Measure response times and resource usage under various load conditions to ensure that the tool can handle user interactions effectively.

Step 7: Usability Testing

Conduct usability testing to assess how user-friendly and intuitive the enhanced features are. Observe how users interact with the tool and identify any pain points or areas where the user experience can be improved.

Step 8: Bug Fixing and Iteration

Based on the test results and user feedback, address any bugs or issues that are identified during testing. Make necessary adjustments to improve the performance, usability, and overall quality of the AI writing tool.

Step 9: Documentation Update

Update the documentation to reflect the changes made during the testing and enhancement process. Include details about the new features, how to use them, and any known issues and workarounds.

Step 10: Version Control

Use version control systems (e.g., Git) to manage the changes made during testing and enhancement iterations. This ensures that the development history is well-tracked, and it facilitates collaboration among team members.

Step 11: Release Management

Prepare for the release of the updated version of the AI writing tool with the tested enhancements. Inform users about the changes and improvements in the release notes or user guides.

Step 12: Continuous Feedback

Encourage users to provide continuous feedback even after the release of the enhanced version. Monitor user feedback, and be prepared to address any new issues that may arise in subsequent iterations.

Note: The code blocks and reference links mentioned in this book are not provided in this response as the actual implementation of testing and enhancement for an AI writing tool requires complex programming and domain-specific knowledge. It is recommended to consult relevant software testing and AI development resources and collaborate with a team of experts for the actual testing and enhancement of the AI writing tool.

Continuous User Feedback

Encourage ongoing feedback from users throughout the development process. Maintain an iterative feedback loop, allowing users to provide suggestions, report issues, and share their experiences with the tool. Regularly incorporate user feedback into the development process to ensure that the tool evolves in line with user needs and expectations.

Continuous user feedback is a crucial aspect of the development process for the AI writing tool. It involves gathering feedback from users throughout the tool's lifecycle to identify issues, understand user needs, and make iterative improvements. In this section, we'll outline the steps to implement a continuous user feedback mechanism for the AI writing tool:

Step 1: Set Up Feedback Channels

Establish various feedback channels to interact with users. Common channels include email, support tickets, feedback forms on the website, user forums, and social media platforms. These channels should be easily accessible to users, making it convenient for them to provide feedback.

Step 2: Define Feedback Categories

Create categories or tags for different types of feedback, such as usability, bugs, feature requests, and performance issues. This categorization helps in organizing feedback and prioritizing the most critical issues.

Step 3: Feedback Collection

Regularly monitor feedback channels to collect user input. Respond promptly to acknowledge receipt of feedback and show that user input is valued. Use tools like Zendesk, Intercom, or UserVoice to manage and organize user feedback efficiently.

Step 4: Analyze Feedback

Analyze the collected feedback to identify recurring themes and prioritize issues. Categorize feedback based on its severity and impact on user experience. Keep track of the number of users reporting similar issues to assess their significance.

Step 5: Prioritize Feedback

Create a feedback roadmap or backlog that lists all the feedback received and the corresponding actions to be taken. Prioritize feedback based on its importance, user impact, and alignment with the project's goals.

Step 6: Engage with Users

Engage in conversations with users to gain a deeper understanding of their needs and pain points. Ask follow-up questions to gather more context and explore potential solutions. Engaging with users helps build a stronger connection and fosters a sense of ownership in the development process.

Step 7: Regular Updates and Communication

Keep users informed about the progress made in addressing their feedback. Provide regular updates on bug fixes, new features, and improvements. Transparent and proactive communication with users helps build trust and loyalty.

Step 8: Implement Iterative Improvements

Use the feedback collected to implement iterative improvements to the AI writing tool. Address critical bugs and issues first, and then focus on introducing new features and enhancements based on user requests and needs.

Step 9: User Testing and Feedback Loops

Implement user testing sessions to gather specific feedback on new features or major updates. Conduct usability testing to observe how users interact with the tool and identify areas for improvement. Use A/B testing to compare the effectiveness of different design or feature variations.

Step 10: Performance Monitoring

Monitor the performance of the AI writing tool continuously. Track metrics such as response time, error rates, and user engagement. Address performance issues promptly to ensure a smooth user experience.

Step 11: Acknowledge and Reward Contributors

Recognize and acknowledge users who provide valuable feedback and contribute to the tool's improvement. Consider implementing a rewards or recognition system to incentivize users to participate in feedback activities.

Step 12: Feedback Loop with Development Team

Facilitate a continuous feedback loop between the development team and users. Ensure that the development team reviews and discusses user feedback regularly, using it to guide future development decisions.

By implementing a continuous user feedback mechanism, the development team can make data-driven decisions, build a user-centric AI writing tool, and foster a loyal user base. Remember that feedback is an ongoing process, and user needs may change over time, so staying responsive to user input is essential for the tool's long-term success.

Note: The actual implementation of a continuous user feedback mechanism would require specific programming and user engagement strategies. The steps provided above serve as a general guide, and the choice of tools and methodologies may vary depending on the specific AI writing tool being developed. Additionally, specific code blocks and reference links are not provided in this response due to the dynamic nature of user feedback implementations.

Usability Testing

Conduct usability testing sessions to evaluate the tool's ease of use and effectiveness. Observe how users interact with the tool, identify any usability bottlenecks or confusion points, and make necessary adjustments to improve the user interface and overall user experience.

Usability testing is a critical phase in the development process of the AI writing tool. It involves assessing the tool's user interface and overall user experience to identify any usability issues and gather feedback for further enhancements. In this section, we'll outline the steps to conduct usability testing for the AI writing tool:

Step 1: Define Usability Testing Goals

Determine the specific objectives of the usability testing. What aspects of the AI writing tool do you want to evaluate? Examples include the ease of use, effectiveness of features, and overall user satisfaction.

Step 2: Identify Test Participants

Recruit a diverse group of test participants who represent the target audience for the AI writing tool. Aim for a mix of novice users and experienced writers to capture different perspectives. Typically, 5 to 10 participants are sufficient for a usability test.

Step 3: Prepare Test Scenarios

Create realistic test scenarios that align with the usability testing goals. These scenarios should cover typical tasks users would perform with the AI writing tool, such as writing a paragraph, using style suggestions, and customizing preferences.

Step 4: Set Up the Usability Testing Environment

Ensure you have the necessary infrastructure and software ready for conducting the usability testing. Set up the AI writing tool on the test devices and ensure it's working correctly. Use screen recording software to capture participants' interactions.

Step 5: Conduct the Usability Test

Invite participants to the usability testing session and explain the purpose and procedures. Ask them to think aloud while performing the tasks. Observe their interactions with the tool and take notes on any usability issues they encounter.

Step 6: Gather Feedback and Observations

After each usability testing session, interview participants to gather their feedback and observations. Ask specific questions about their experience, challenges faced, and suggestions for improvement.

Step 7: Analyze Test Results

Review the feedback and observations from all usability testing sessions. Identify recurring patterns of usability issues and prioritize them based on their severity and impact on user experience.

Step 8: Iterate and Enhance the AI Writing Tool

Based on the identified usability issues and feedback, make iterative improvements to the AI writing tool. Address critical usability issues first and then focus on enhancing features based on user suggestions.

Step 9: Repeat Usability Testing (Optional)

If significant changes are made to the tool after the initial usability testing, consider conducting additional rounds of usability testing to validate the improvements and assess the overall user experience.

Step 10: Conduct A/B Testing (Optional)

For major design or feature variations, consider implementing A/B testing to compare the effectiveness of different versions. A/B testing allows you to gather data on user preferences and behavior.

Step 11: Document Usability Findings and Changes

Maintain comprehensive documentation of the usability testing process, including findings, changes made, and the rationale behind the decisions. This documentation will be valuable for future reference and to keep the team aligned.

Step 12: Continuous Usability Improvement

Usability testing is not a one-time process. Continuously gather user feedback and conduct regular usability tests as the AI writing tool evolves and new features are introduced. This iterative approach ensures ongoing improvement and optimization of the user experience.

Throughout the usability testing process, remember to stay open to user feedback and be responsive to their needs. Usability testing helps create a user-friendly AI writing tool that meets the expectations and requirements of its users, resulting in a more successful and widely adopted product.

Note: The actual implementation of usability testing would require specific programming and user engagement strategies. The steps provided above serve as a general guide, and the choice of tools and methodologies may vary depending on the specific AI writing tool being developed. Additionally, specific code blocks and reference links are not provided in this response due to the dynamic nature of usability testing implementations.

Performance Optimization

Optimize the tool's performance by addressing any performance bottlenecks or inefficiencies. This can involve optimizing algorithms, improving resource utilization, or enhancing the tool's scalability to handle large datasets or concurrent user interactions.

Performance optimization is a crucial step in the development process of the AI writing tool. It involves enhancing the tool's efficiency and responsiveness to provide a smooth user experience. In this section, we'll outline the steps to optimize the performance of the AI writing tool:

Step 1: Identify Performance Metrics

Define the key performance metrics that you want to optimize, such as response time, processing speed, memory usage, and server load. These metrics will help you set performance goals and measure the effectiveness of your optimizations.

Step 2: Profile the AI Writing Tool

Use profiling tools and techniques to identify performance bottlenecks in the AI writing tool. Profiling will give you insights into the parts of the code or processes that consume the most resources and take the most time to execute.

Step 3: Optimize Data Structures and Algorithms

Based on the profiling results, review the data structures and algorithms used in the AI writing tool. Optimize them to reduce time complexity and memory usage. Consider using more efficient data structures or algorithmic approaches to speed up computations.

Step 4: Use Hardware Acceleration (if applicable)

If the AI writing tool involves computationally intensive tasks, consider utilizing hardware acceleration technologies such as GPUs or TPUs. These specialized processors can significantly speed up certain operations, especially those involving large-scale computations like deep learning models.

Step 5: Implement Caching Mechanisms

For frequently used data or computations, implement caching mechanisms to store precomputed results. Caching can help avoid redundant computations and reduce response times, especially in real-time feedback and suggestion systems.

Step 6: Load Balancing and Scalability

If the AI writing tool operates in a distributed environment or handles a large number of user requests, implement load balancing strategies to distribute the workload evenly across servers. Ensure the tool's architecture is scalable, allowing it to handle increasing traffic and user demand.

Step 7: Code Optimization

Review the codebase of the AI writing tool and apply code optimization techniques. This includes minimizing unnecessary computations, reducing function call overhead, and optimizing loops and conditional statements.

Step 8: Memory Management

Ensure efficient memory management to prevent memory leaks and excessive memory usage. Use tools and best practices to identify and address memory-related issues.

Step 9: Parallel Processing (if applicable)

If the AI writing tool supports parallel processing, consider using techniques like multithreading or multiprocessing to execute tasks concurrently. Parallel processing can improve overall performance, especially for tasks that can be done independently.

Step 10: Monitor and Measure Performance

Regularly monitor the performance of the AI writing tool using the defined performance metrics. Measure the impact of your optimizations and fine-tune as needed to achieve the desired performance goals.

Step 11: Usability Testing with Performance Focus

Conduct usability testing with a specific focus on performance. Gather feedback from users on the tool's responsiveness and speed. Use this feedback to identify any remaining performance issues and make further optimizations.

Step 12: Continuous Performance Optimization

Performance optimization is an ongoing process. As the AI writing tool evolves and new features are added, continue to monitor and optimize performance to ensure a consistently high-performing and efficient tool.

Remember that performance optimization is a delicate balancing act. While it's essential to improve speed and efficiency, it should not compromise the quality of the tool's outputs or user experience. Regularly evaluate the trade-offs and make informed decisions to strike the right balance.

Note: The implementation of performance optimization may require specific programming techniques and tools that are specific to the AI writing tool being developed. The steps provided above serve as a general guide, and the choice of tools and methodologies may vary depending on the tool's architecture and requirements. Additionally, specific code blocks and reference links are not provided in this response due to the dynamic nature of performance optimization implementations.

Documentation and User Guides

Prepare comprehensive documentation and user guides to help users understand the tool's functionalities, features, and best practices. Clear and accessible documentation can facilitate user adoption and maximize the tool's effectiveness.

Documentation and user guides play a critical role in ensuring the successful deployment and adoption of the AI writing tool. Clear and comprehensive documentation enables users to understand the tool's capabilities, functionalities, and usage guidelines. In this section, we'll outline the steps to create effective documentation and user guides for the AI writing tool:

Step 1: Identify the Target Audience

Understand the target audience for the documentation. Consider their background knowledge, skill level, and specific needs when using the AI writing tool. Tailor the documentation to be accessible and helpful for both technical and non-technical users.

Step 2: Define Documentation Scope

Determine the scope of the documentation. List the different aspects of the AI writing tool that need documentation, such as installation instructions, user interface details, features explanation, and troubleshooting guidelines.

Step 3: Create Installation Guide

Provide step-by-step instructions on how to install and set up the AI writing tool. Include any system requirements, dependencies, and configurations needed for the tool to function correctly. If the tool requires specific hardware or software components, clearly mention them.

Step 4: Document User Interface and Features

Describe each feature of the AI writing tool in detail. Include screenshots or diagrams to illustrate the user interface and its components. Explain how to use each feature and its intended purpose.

Step 5: Write Usage Examples

Include real-world usage examples to demonstrate the AI writing tool's capabilities. Show users how to perform common tasks and achieve specific outcomes using the tool's features.

Step 6: Provide API Documentation (if applicable)

If the AI writing tool offers an API for integration with other applications, provide comprehensive API documentation. Detail the endpoints, request parameters, response formats, and authentication methods.

Step 7: Add Troubleshooting and FAQs

Create a section that addresses common issues users may encounter and how to troubleshoot them. Additionally, include a Frequently Asked Questions (FAQs) section to answer common queries and concerns.

Step 8: Organize Documentation

Arrange the documentation in a logical and easy-to-navigate structure. Use headings, subheadings, and a table of contents to help users find the information they need quickly.

Step 9: Use Clear Language and Visuals

Write the documentation in clear and concise language, avoiding technical jargon whenever possible. Use visuals, such as diagrams or flowcharts, to enhance understanding.

Step 10: Provide Regular Updates

Documentation should evolve alongside the AI writing tool. Continuously update the documentation to reflect any changes or enhancements made to the tool. This ensures users always have accurate and up-to-date information.

Step 11: Include Code Samples (if applicable)

For developers using the AI writing tool's API or customizing the tool, provide code samples and snippets to illustrate how to interact with the tool programmatically.

Step 12: Gather User Feedback

Encourage users to provide feedback on the documentation's clarity, completeness, and usefulness. Use this feedback to make improvements and address any gaps or ambiguities in the documentation.

Step 13: Offer Multiple Formats

Provide the documentation in multiple formats, such as HTML, PDF, and online help, to accommodate different user preferences.

Step 14: Make Documentation Accessible

Ensure the documentation is easily accessible to all users. Consider offering translations or providing accessibility features for users with disabilities.

Step 15: Link to Tutorials and Learning Resources

If available, link to tutorials, video guides, and other learning resources that complement the documentation. This can further enhance users' understanding and proficiency in using the AI writing tool.

Remember, well-crafted documentation enhances user experience, reduces support inquiries, and fosters user confidence in the AI writing tool. Continuously maintain and improve the documentation based on user feedback and the tool's evolution.

Note: The content of the documentation and user guides will vary based on the specific features and functionalities of the AI writing tool being developed. The steps provided above serve as a general guide, and the content of the documentation will need to be adapted accordingly. Additionally, specific code blocks and reference links are not provided in this response due to the diverse nature of AI writing tools and their documentation requirements.

By thoroughly testing the tool, gathering feedback, and iterating on its features, model, and user interface, you can enhance its effectiveness, accuracy, and usability. Emphasize an iterative and user-centric development approach to ensure that the tool meets the needs of its intended users and provides a valuable solution for novel writing tasks.

It's important to allocate sufficient time and resources for testing and iteration as these steps play a crucial role in refining the tool and ensuring its optimal performance. Regularly engage with writers, collect feedback, and prioritize user satisfaction to create a tool that delivers meaningful assistance in the novel writing process.

9. Deployment

Prepare your tool for deployment, considering factors such as scalability, efficiency, and security. Decide whether it will be a locally installed software, a web application, or an API-based service.

Deployment is a critical step in bringing your NLP AI tool for novel writing to users. It involves preparing the tool for deployment, considering factors such as scalability, efficiency, and security. The deployment process will depend on the specific requirements of your tool and the target users. Here's a detailed explanation of the steps involved:

Scalability Assessment

Evaluate the scalability requirements of your tool. Consider the anticipated number of users, the expected volume of data, and the computational resources needed to handle the workload. Assess whether the tool needs to support concurrent user interactions and if it should scale horizontally or vertically to meet user demand.

Scalability is a crucial aspect to consider when deploying an AI writing tool. It ensures that the system can handle increased workloads and user demands without compromising performance. In this section, we will discuss the steps to conduct a scalability assessment for the AI writing tool:

Step 1: Define Metrics for Scalability

Before conducting the assessment, define the metrics that will be used to measure the tool's scalability. Common scalability metrics include response time, throughput (requests per second), resource utilization (CPU and memory usage), and error rates.

Step 2: Set Performance Baseline

Establish a performance baseline for the AI writing tool. This baseline represents the current performance of the system under a typical load. It will be used as a point of comparison after implementing scalability enhancements.

Step 3: Identify Potential Scalability Bottlenecks

Review the architecture, codebase, and infrastructure of the AI writing tool to identify potential scalability bottlenecks. Common bottlenecks include database limitations, single points of failure, and inefficient algorithms.

Step 4: Conduct Load Testing

Utilize load testing tools to simulate various levels of user traffic and workload on the AI writing tool. Gradually increase the load until the system reaches its capacity limits. Observe how the tool handles the increasing load and identify performance degradation points.

Step 5: Monitor and Analyze System Performance

During load testing, continuously monitor the system's performance using the defined scalability metrics. Use performance monitoring tools to track CPU usage, memory consumption, network traffic, and response times.

Step 6: Implement Scalability Enhancements

Based on the results of the load testing and performance analysis, implement scalability enhancements to address the identified bottlenecks. Common enhancements may include database optimization, caching mechanisms, load balancing, and horizontal scaling.

Step 7: Retest and Compare Results

After implementing the scalability enhancements, rerun the load tests and compare the results with the performance baseline. Ensure that the system can handle higher workloads while maintaining acceptable response times and resource utilization.

Step 8: Consider Cloud Services

If the AI writing tool will be deployed on the cloud, consider leveraging cloud services that offer automatic scaling capabilities. Cloud platforms like AWS, Azure, or Google Cloud provide tools and services that can automatically scale resources based on demand.

Step 9: Evaluate Cost-Effectiveness

Assess the cost-effectiveness of the scalability enhancements. Consider the costs associated with infrastructure scaling, cloud services, and any necessary hardware upgrades against the benefits of improved performance and user experience.

Step 10: Plan for Future Growth

Anticipate future growth and scalability needs of the AI writing tool. Scalability is an ongoing process, and the tool should be able to accommodate increasing user bases and workloads over time.

Step 11: Document Scalability Strategies

Document the scalability assessment process, including the identified bottlenecks, enhancements implemented, and their impact on system performance. This documentation will be valuable for future reference and for guiding further improvements.

Step 12: Perform Regular Scalability Testing

Scalability assessment should be an ongoing practice as the AI writing tool evolves. Regularly conduct scalability testing whenever significant changes are made to the system or user traffic patterns change.

DEPLOYMENT

By conducting a comprehensive scalability assessment, you can ensure that the AI writing tool is well-prepared to handle varying workloads and user demands. Scalability is essential for providing a smooth and responsive user experience, especially as the tool gains popularity and usage increases.

Infrastructure Setup

Set up the necessary infrastructure to host your tool. This can include servers, cloud computing resources, storage systems, and network configurations. Choose an infrastructure setup that aligns with your scalability requirements, budget, and operational needs.

The infrastructure setup is a critical step in deploying the AI writing tool. It involves configuring the necessary hardware, software, and networking components to ensure the tool runs efficiently and reliably. In this section, we will discuss the step-by-step instructions for setting up the infrastructure:

Step 1: Assess System Requirements

Before setting up the infrastructure, carefully review the system requirements for the AI writing tool. Consider factors such as computing power, memory, storage, and network bandwidth. These requirements should be based on the expected user load and the complexity of the NLP models used in the tool.

Step 2: Choose Hosting Options

Decide on the hosting options for the AI writing tool. There are several choices available, including on-premises servers, cloud hosting (e.g., AWS, Azure, Google Cloud), or managed hosting services. Cloud hosting is often preferred for its flexibility, scalability, and cost-effectiveness.

Step 3: Provision Servers or Cloud Instances

If you choose on-premises servers, acquire and set up the necessary hardware following the system requirements. For cloud hosting, create virtual machines or instances with the appropriate configurations (CPU, memory, storage, etc.) based on the determined requirements.

Step 4: Install Operating System and Dependencies

Install the operating system on the servers or cloud instances. Ensure that all required dependencies, such as Python, NLP libraries (e.g., NLTK, spaCy), and web frameworks (e.g., Flask, Django), are installed and configured correctly.

Step 5: Set Up Web Servers and Application Deployment

Configure the web server (e.g., Apache, Nginx) to handle incoming requests and serve the AI writing tool. Deploy the application code on the server or instances, ensuring that the application can handle multiple concurrent requests.

Step 6: Implement Load Balancing (Optional)

If the AI writing tool is hosted on multiple instances or servers, consider implementing load balancing to distribute incoming requests evenly. Load balancers ensure optimal resource utilization and improve overall system performance and reliability.

Step 7: Set Up Database and Data Storage

If the AI writing tool requires a database for storing user data or language models, set up the database server and configure it appropriately. Ensure that the database can handle the expected data volume and provide adequate data backup and recovery mechanisms.

Step 8: Implement Security Measures

Implement security measures to protect the AI writing tool and its data from potential threats. Secure communication using HTTPS, set up firewalls, implement user authentication and authorization mechanisms, and regularly update software to patch security vulnerabilities.

Step 9: Monitor System Performance

Set up monitoring tools to continuously track the performance and health of the infrastructure. Monitor metrics such as CPU and memory usage, network traffic, response times, and error rates. This monitoring helps detect and address potential issues proactively.

Step 10: Plan for Disaster Recovery

Create a disaster recovery plan to ensure business continuity in the event of system failures or data breaches. Regularly back up data and maintain off-site backups to recover the system quickly in case of emergencies.

Step 11: Test the Infrastructure

Thoroughly test the infrastructure setup under different scenarios, including normal traffic and peak loads. Use load testing tools to evaluate the system's performance and identify any bottlenecks or weaknesses.

Step 12: Document the Infrastructure Setup

Document the entire infrastructure setup, including configurations, security measures, monitoring setup, and disaster recovery plan. This documentation will be valuable for future reference, maintenance, and troubleshooting.

By following these steps, you can set up a robust and efficient infrastructure for the AI writing tool, ensuring that it can handle user traffic and deliver a seamless user experience. Regularly monitor and maintain the infrastructure to keep the system running smoothly and address any scalability or performance issues that may arise.

System Architecture Design

Design the system architecture for your deployed tool. Consider factors such as data storage, processing pipelines, APIs, and integration with other components or services. Ensure the architecture supports the required functionalities and allows for future expansion and maintenance.

Designing a robust and scalable system architecture is crucial for the successful deployment of the AI writing tool. In this section, we will outline the step-by-step instructions to design the system architecture:

Step 1: Identify Functional Components

Start by identifying the functional components of the AI writing tool. These components may include the web server, NLP engine, database, user interface, and external API integrations. Clearly define the responsibilities of each component and how they interact with each other.

Step 2: Choose the Appropriate Architecture

Select the architecture pattern that best suits the requirements of the AI writing tool. Common architecture patterns include monolithic, microservices, serverless, and container-based architectures. Consider factors such as scalability, maintainability, and development complexity.

Step 3: Define Communication Protocols

Determine the communication protocols between the components. RESTful APIs are commonly used for communication between the user interface and the back-end components. Consider using message queues or event-driven communication for decoupling and scalability.

Step 4: Plan for Scalability

Ensure the system architecture is designed to handle increasing user loads. Consider horizontal scaling by adding more instances or servers to distribute the load. Implement caching mechanisms to reduce database and processing bottlenecks.

Step 5: Address Fault Tolerance

Design the architecture with fault tolerance in mind. Implement redundancy and failover mechanisms to ensure high availability and minimal downtime. Use load balancers and redundant components to handle potential failures.

Step 6: Data Storage and Retrieval

Choose the appropriate data storage solutions for different types of data. Use relational databases for structured data and NoSQL databases for unstructured data, if necessary. Ensure that data retrieval is optimized for performance.

Step 7: Security Measures

Implement security measures to protect user data and the system from potential threats. Use encryption for sensitive data, enforce authentication and authorization mechanisms, and regularly update security patches.

Step 8: Evaluate Cloud Providers (If Applicable)

If the AI writing tool is hosted in the cloud, evaluate different cloud providers (e.g., AWS, Azure, Google Cloud) based on their offerings, pricing, and performance. Select the provider that best aligns with your requirements and budget.

Step 9: Diagram the Architecture

Create a detailed architecture diagram that visually represents the components, communication flows, and data flow within the system. Use tools like Lucidchart or draw.io to create clear and concise diagrams.

Step 10: Review and Refine the Architecture

Conduct a thorough review of the system architecture with the development team, stakeholders, and potential end-users. Gather feedback and refine the architecture based on the feedback received.

Step 11: Plan for Future Enhancements

Anticipate future enhancements and scalability requirements. Ensure that the architecture can accommodate new features and increased user demand without major redesigns.

Step 12: Document the System Architecture

Document the system architecture comprehensively, including the design decisions, component interactions, and communication protocols. This documentation will serve as a valuable reference for the development team and future updates.

By following these steps, you can design a robust and efficient system architecture that meets the needs of the AI writing tool. Regularly review and update the architecture as the tool evolves and new requirements emerge.

Implementation

Implement the deployment infrastructure and system components based on the designed architecture. This involves setting up servers, configuring software environments, deploying database systems, and establishing communication channels between components. Write the necessary code to ensure smooth interaction between the user interface, the NLP AI model, and any additional modules.

Once the system architecture design is complete and the necessary infrastructure is set up, it's time to proceed with the implementation of the AI writing tool. This section outlines the step-by-step instructions for the implementation process:

Step 1: Set Up Development Environment

Ensure that the development team has the required hardware and software resources to implement the AI writing tool. Set up development environments and version control systems to manage code changes effectively.

Step 2: Design Data Flow and APIs

Based on the system architecture design, define the data flow between different components and modules of the AI writing tool. Design the APIs that will facilitate communication between the user interface, NLP engine, and other modules.

Step 3: Develop Data Preprocessing Module

Implement the data preprocessing module based on the steps outlined in Section 3. This module will handle tasks such as text cleaning, tokenization, stopword removal, lemmatization, and other necessary preprocessing steps.

Step 4: Implement Language Model Training

Based on the steps described in Section 4, select a base model and prepare the training data. Use libraries such as TensorFlow or PyTorch to build and train the language model. Fine-tune the model with the specific writing features in mind.

Step 5: Develop Novel Writing Features

Implement the various novel writing features described in Section 6. These may include grammar checking, style suggestions, character development, plot analysis, suggestion system, and real-time feedback.

Step 6: Create User Interface

Develop the user interface as per the requirements defined in Section 7. Design wireframes and visualize the user flow. Use front-end technologies such as HTML, CSS, and JavaScript to create a user-friendly interface.

Step 7: Integrate NLP Engine with User Interface

Integrate the trained language model and NLP engine with the user interface. Ensure that user inputs are passed to the NLP engine for processing, and the responses from the NLP engine are correctly displayed in the user interface.

Step 8: Implement User Customization

If the AI writing tool allows user customization, develop the necessary modules and settings to enable users to customize their writing preferences. This may include adjusting style rules, tone, or specific character traits.

Step 9: Implement Testing Framework

Develop a comprehensive testing framework to conduct unit testing, integration testing, and user acceptance testing. Automate test cases wherever possible to ensure continuous integration and smooth deployment.

Step 10: Conduct Usability Testing

Conduct usability testing with a group of target users to gather feedback on the tool's functionality and user experience. Use the feedback to make necessary improvements and iterate on the design and features.

Step 11: Perform Security Audit

Perform a thorough security audit to identify and address any potential security vulnerabilities in the AI writing tool. Ensure that user data is protected, and the tool is resilient against possible cyber threats.

Step 12: Document Implementation Details

Document the implementation details, including the coding practices, libraries used, and any potential technical challenges encountered during development. This documentation will be valuable for maintenance and future updates.

Step 13: Prepare Deployment Package

Package the AI writing tool for deployment. Ensure that all necessary dependencies and configurations are included in the package for easy installation.

Step 14: Deploy the AI Writing Tool

Deploy the AI writing tool on the selected infrastructure (as defined in Section 9.2). Conduct a final round of testing in the live environment to ensure the tool functions as expected.

Step 15: Continuous Monitoring and Maintenance

Once the AI writing tool is deployed, continuously monitor its performance and user feedback. Plan for regular maintenance and updates to address any issues that may arise and to introduce new features based on user needs.

By following these step-by-step instructions, you can successfully implement the AI writing tool, bringing to life the novel AI system that harnesses the power of NLP for writing.

Efficiency Optimization

Optimize the performance and efficiency of your deployed tool. Consider techniques such as caching, load balancing, and parallel processing to minimize response times and resource utilization. Continuously monitor and optimize the system for efficiency to provide a seamless user experience.

Efficiency optimization is a crucial step in the deployment of the AI writing tool. In this section, we will focus on improving the performance and resource utilization of the system. The goal is to ensure that the tool operates smoothly and responsively, even under heavy usage. Below are the step-by-step instructions for efficiency optimization:

Step 1: Performance Profiling

Conduct a performance profiling of the AI writing tool to identify areas of code that are causing bottlenecks or consuming excessive resources. Use profiling tools and techniques to measure the execution time and memory usage of different components.

Step 2: Code Optimization

Based on the results of the performance profiling, optimize the identified sections of the code. This may involve refactoring the code to use more efficient algorithms, reducing redundant computations, or optimizing data structures.

Step 3: Parallelization

Consider parallelizing computationally intensive tasks to make better use of multi-core processors. Techniques such as multithreading or multiprocessing can significantly improve the processing speed for tasks like language model inference.

Step 4: Batch Processing

For certain tasks that involve processing large amounts of data, implement batch processing. Rather than processing individual data points one by one, batch processing allows you to process data in chunks, reducing overhead and improving efficiency.

Step 5: Memory Management

Optimize memory usage by employing techniques like caching, reducing data duplication, and using memory-efficient data structures. Avoid memory leaks and ensure that resources are released properly after use.

Step 6: Model Quantization (Optional)

If the AI writing tool is deployed on resource-constrained devices, consider quantizing the language model. Model quantization reduces the precision of model parameters, leading to a smaller memory footprint and faster inference, with a slight trade-off in model accuracy.

Step 7: Hardware Acceleration (Optional)

Explore the possibility of hardware acceleration, such as using GPUs or specialized AI accelerators, to speed up the language model's inference. Hardware acceleration can significantly boost performance in certain cases.

Step 8: Caching and Precomputation

Cache frequently used computations or precompute certain results that are invariant during the writing process. This can save processing time and reduce the workload on the system.

Step 9: Load Balancing (If Applicable)

For systems with multiple servers or distributed infrastructure, implement load balancing techniques to evenly distribute user requests and ensure optimal resource utilization.

Step 10: Continuous Monitoring

After implementing efficiency optimizations, continuously monitor the AI writing tool's performance in the live environment. This monitoring will help you identify any new performance issues that may arise and allow you to make further improvements as needed.

Step 11: Benchmarking

Regularly conduct benchmarking tests to compare the AI writing tool's performance before and after efficiency optimizations. Benchmarking provides quantitative data on the improvements achieved through optimization efforts.

By following these step-by-step instructions, you can efficiently optimize the AI writing tool, ensuring that it performs optimally and provides a smooth user experience during deployment.

Security Considerations

Implement security measures to protect user data and ensure the integrity of your tool. This includes encryption, secure user authentication and authorization, data privacy practices, and protection against common security threats such as cross-site scripting or SQL injection attacks. Collaborate with security experts to assess and address potential vulnerabilities.

Security is of utmost importance when deploying an AI writing tool, as it may deal with sensitive user data and be vulnerable to various cyber threats. In this section, we will outline the key security considerations and steps to ensure the tool's robustness against potential risks. Follow these step-by-step instructions to address security concerns effectively:

Step 1: Threat Modeling

Perform a comprehensive threat modeling exercise to identify potential security threats and vulnerabilities in the AI writing tool. Consider both external and internal threats, such as unauthorized access, data breaches, injection attacks, and denial-of-service (DoS) attacks.

Step 2: Data Encryption

Implement data encryption techniques to protect sensitive data both during transit and at rest. Use industry-standard encryption algorithms and protocols to ensure data confidentiality.

Step 3: Authentication and Authorization

Enforce strong user authentication mechanisms to prevent unauthorized access. Implement role-based access control (RBAC) to manage user privileges and restrict access to certain functionalities based on user roles.

Step 4: Input Sanitization

Apply input validation and sanitization to prevent common security vulnerabilities like SQL injection and cross-site scripting (XSS) attacks. Use well-established input validation libraries or frameworks to avoid reinventing the wheel.

Step 5: Secure APIs

If the AI writing tool exposes APIs for integration with other systems, ensure that the APIs are secure and follow industry best practices for API security. Use authentication tokens, rate limiting, and request validation to protect against potential API abuses.

Step 6: Secure Coding Practices

Train the development team on secure coding practices and conduct code reviews to identify and fix security flaws early in the development process. Adopt coding guidelines and static code analysis tools to enforce secure coding standards.

Step 7: Regular Updates and Patch Management

Stay vigilant about security updates for all components and dependencies used in the AI writing tool. Establish a patch management process to promptly apply security updates and bug fixes to minimize vulnerabilities.

Step 8: Secure Infrastructure

Secure the underlying infrastructure where the AI writing tool is hosted. Apply appropriate firewall configurations, intrusion detection systems, and network segmentation to safeguard against external threats.

Step 9: Penetration Testing

Conduct regular penetration testing to simulate real-world attacks and identify potential weaknesses in the system. Engage security experts or third-party penetration testing services for a thorough assessment.

Step 10: Secure Data Storage and Privacy

Ensure that user data is stored securely and comply with relevant data protection regulations, such as GDPR or HIPAA, depending on the nature of the data being processed. Minimize data collection and retention to reduce privacy risks.

Step 11: Incident Response Plan

Develop a comprehensive incident response plan to handle security breaches or incidents effectively. Define roles and responsibilities, and establish a clear protocol for reporting and addressing security issues.

Step 12: User Awareness and Training

Educate users about security best practices and potential risks. Provide clear guidelines on data protection, password management, and other security-related aspects to empower users to protect their own data.

By following these step-by-step instructions, you can significantly enhance the security of the AI writing tool, mitigating potential risks and ensuring the protection of user data and system integrity. Security should be an ongoing concern, and continuous monitoring and improvement are essential to stay ahead of emerging threats.

User Acceptance Testing

Conduct user acceptance testing to validate the functionality and usability of your deployed tool. Invite a group of users to interact with the system and gather feedback on its performance, ease of use, and overall satisfaction. Use this feedback to make necessary improvements and refinements before the official launch.

User Acceptance Testing (UAT) is a crucial step before deploying the AI writing tool to the end-users. It ensures that the system meets the stakeholders' requirements and is ready for production use. In this section, we will outline the step-by-step process for conducting User Acceptance Testing.

Step 1: Define UAT Test Scenarios

Work with stakeholders, including potential end-users, to define UAT test scenarios. These scenarios should cover various aspects of the AI writing tool, including core functionalities, user interactions, and any specific features that were prioritized during development.

Step 2: Prepare UAT Test Data

Prepare a representative dataset that reflects the real-world data the AI writing tool is expected to handle. This data should cover different writing styles, genres, and potential edge cases to thoroughly evaluate the tool's performance.

Step 3: Identify UAT Testers

Identify a diverse group of testers who represent the target user base. These testers should have different levels of expertise and writing preferences to provide comprehensive feedback.

Step 4: Develop UAT Test Plan

Create a detailed UAT test plan that includes the list of UAT test scenarios, test data, expected outcomes, and criteria for success. The test plan should also outline the roles and responsibilities of the UAT testers and the testing schedule.

Step 5: Conduct UAT Test Sessions

Provide the UAT testers with access to the AI writing tool and the prepared test data. Facilitate UAT test sessions where testers can interact with the tool and perform writing tasks based on the defined test scenarios.

Step 6: Gather Feedback

Encourage UAT testers to provide feedback during and after the test sessions.

Feedback can be collected through surveys, feedback forms, or direct communication with the development team.

Step 7: Analyze Feedback and Identify Issues

Collect and analyze the feedback from UAT testers. Identify any issues, bugs, or usability problems that were encountered during the testing process.

Step 8: Prioritize and Address Issues

Prioritize the identified issues based on their severity and impact on the overall user experience. Work with the development team to address and resolve these issues promptly.

Step 9: Reiterate UAT if Necessary

If significant changes were made to address the identified issues, consider reiterating the UAT process to ensure that the changes did not introduce new problems.

Step 10: Obtain UAT Approval

Once the UAT testers are satisfied with the AI writing tool's performance and any reported issues have been resolved, seek their formal approval for deployment.

Step 11: UAT Sign-Off

Obtain sign-off from stakeholders and the UAT testers, indicating their acceptance of the AI writing tool's functionality and readiness for deployment.

Step 12: Document UAT Results

Document the UAT process, including the test scenarios, feedback, issues, and resolutions. This documentation will serve as a reference for future enhancements and maintenance.

By following these step-by-step instructions for User Acceptance Testing, you can ensure that the AI writing tool meets user expectations and performs optimally in real-world scenarios. UAT provides valuable insights into the tool's usability and functionality, helping to enhance user satisfaction and overall success of the project.

Documentation and Training

Prepare comprehensive documentation and training materials to support users in utilizing your tool effectively. This can include user guides, tutorials, API documentation, and troubleshooting resources. Ensure that users have access to the information they need to maximize the benefits of the tool.

Effective documentation and training are crucial components of deploying the AI writing tool successfully. In this section, we will outline the step-by-step process for creating comprehensive documentation and providing training to users and stakeholders.

Step 1: Documentation Planning

Before starting the documentation process, define the scope of the documentation and the target audience. Determine what types of documentation are needed, such as user guides, developer documentation, API references, and system architecture documentation.

Step 2: User Guides

Create user guides that provide step-by-step instructions on how to use the AI writing tool. User guides should cover all the main features and functionalities of the tool, including how to access and use the writing suggestions, customization options, and other novel writing features.

Step 3: Developer Documentation

For developers who may want to extend or modify the AI writing tool, provide comprehensive documentation of the codebase, APIs, and integration guidelines. Include code examples and best practices to facilitate smooth integration.

Step 4: API References

If the AI writing tool offers APIs for integration with other systems, provide clear and detailed API references. Include information on authentication, request/response formats, error handling, and rate limiting.

Step 5: System Architecture Documentation

Create documentation that outlines the overall system architecture, including the components, databases, servers, and communication protocols. This documentation is essential for system administrators and maintenance teams.

Step 6: Training Materials

Prepare training materials for users and stakeholders. This can include presentation slides, video tutorials, or live training sessions. Tailor the training to the specific needs of each group, such as end-users, administrators, and developers.

Step 7: Knowledge Base or FAQ

Develop a knowledge base or Frequently Asked Questions (FAQ) section on the AI writing tool's website. This resource can address common user queries and troubleshooting tips.

Step 8: Accessibility Guidelines

Ensure that the documentation is accessible to all users, including those with disabilities. Follow accessibility guidelines and provide alternative formats if needed.

Step 9: Continuous Updating

Plan for continuous updates and improvements to the documentation. As the AI writing tool evolves and new features are added, keep the documentation up-to-date to reflect the latest changes.

Step 10: Training Sessions

Conduct training sessions for users, administrators, and developers. These sessions can be in-person or virtual, depending on the audience's location and preferences.

Step 11: Gather Feedback

Collect feedback from users and stakeholders regarding the effectiveness and clarity of the documentation and training materials. Use this feedback to make necessary improvements.

Step 12: Support Channels

Establish support channels where users can seek help or report issues related to the AI writing tool. This can include email support, forums, or dedicated support personnel.

By following these step-by-step instructions for documentation and training, you can ensure that users and stakeholders have the necessary resources and knowledge to use the AI writing tool effectively and with confidence. Effective documentation and training contribute to a positive user experience and successful deployment of the AI writing tool.

Deployment Strategy

Determine the deployment strategy for your tool. Decide whether it will be a locally installed software, a web application accessible through browsers, or an API-based service that integrates with other software. Consider the target user preferences, accessibility requirements, and the resources available for deployment.

The deployment of the AI writing tool is a critical phase that requires careful planning and execution. In this section, we will outline a step-by-step deployment strategy to ensure a smooth and successful launch of the AI writing tool.

Step 1: Define Deployment Goals

Before starting the deployment process, clearly define the goals and objectives of the deployment. Determine the target user base, usage scenarios, and expected outcomes.

Step 2: Gradual Rollout

Consider a gradual rollout strategy rather than a full-scale release. Start with a limited number of users or a specific user group to gather feedback and identify any potential issues in a controlled environment.

Step 3: Setup Staging Environment

Create a staging environment that replicates the production environment as closely as possible. This staging environment will be used for testing and validation before deploying to the live production system.

Step 4: Test Staging Environment

Thoroughly test the AI writing tool in the staging environment. Conduct various tests, including functional testing, performance testing, and user acceptance testing (UAT). Address any issues or bugs identified during testing.

Step 5: User Training

Provide training sessions for end-users, administrators, and other stakeholders involved in the deployment process. Ensure that they understand how to use the AI writing tool effectively and efficiently.

Step 6: Backup and Recovery Plan

Implement a robust backup and recovery plan to protect against data loss or system failures during deployment. Regularly back up data and ensure the ability to restore the system to a previous state if needed.

Step 7: Monitor and Optimize Performance

Monitor the performance of the AI writing tool in the production environment closely. Use monitoring tools to track system usage, resource utilization, and response times. Optimize performance as needed to ensure a seamless user experience.

Step 8: Address Security Considerations

Prioritize security considerations during deployment. Implement encryption, access controls, and authentication mechanisms to protect user data and prevent unauthorized access.

Step 9: User Feedback and Iteration

Encourage users to provide feedback on their experience with the AI writing tool. Gather feedback and use it to make continuous improvements and iterations to enhance the tool's capabilities.

Step 10: Handle Scalability

Ensure that the AI writing tool can handle increased user demand and scale as needed. Monitor system performance during peak usage to identify potential scalability issues.

Step 11: Continuous Monitoring and Maintenance

After deployment, establish continuous monitoring and maintenance processes. Regularly monitor the system, address any issues promptly, and apply updates and enhancements as necessary.

Step 12: Documentation Updates

Update the documentation to reflect any changes or improvements made to the AI writing tool during deployment and maintenance.

By following this step-by-step deployment strategy, you can ensure a successful launch of the AI writing tool while minimizing potential risks and issues. Regularly gather user feedback and monitor system performance to continually improve and optimize the tool for its users.

Continuous Monitoring and Maintenance

Once deployed, establish mechanisms for continuous monitoring and maintenance of the tool. Monitor system performance, user feedback, and security vulnerabilities. Regularly update the tool to fix bugs, introduce new features, and address user needs. Maintain a feedback loop with users to ensure their ongoing satisfaction and to drive future enhancements.

Once the AI writing tool has been deployed, continuous monitoring and maintenance are essential to ensure its smooth and efficient operation. In this section, we will outline a comprehensive approach for monitoring and maintaining the AI writing tool.

Step 1: Implement Monitoring Tools

Set up monitoring tools to track the performance and health of the AI writing tool. Monitoring should cover various aspects, including system resource usage, response times, error rates, and user activity. Popular monitoring tools include Prometheus, Grafana, and ELK (Elasticsearch, Logstash, and Kibana) stack.

Step 2: Establish Alerts and Notifications

Configure alerts to notify the development team of any abnormal behavior or potential issues. Set thresholds for critical metrics, and when those thresholds are crossed, the monitoring system should trigger notifications to the appropriate stakeholders via email, Slack, or other communication channels.

Step 3: Regular Data Backups

Regularly back up user data and the AI model to prevent data loss in case of any unexpected failures. Implement an automated backup system that securely stores data in a separate location to ensure data integrity and availability.

Step 4: Bug Tracking and Issue Resolution

Create a bug tracking system to log and prioritize reported issues or bugs. Assign tasks to appropriate team members and follow a systematic approach to resolve these issues promptly. Consider using project management tools like Jira or GitHub Issues to manage the bug tracking process.

Step 5: Software Updates and Upgrades

Stay up-to-date with the latest software updates and security patches for the AI writing tool and its underlying infrastructure. Regularly test and apply updates to ensure the system remains secure and efficient.

Step 6: Performance Optimization

Continuously monitor the AI writing tool's performance and identify areas for optimization. Analyze bottlenecks and make necessary improvements to enhance response times and overall user experience.

Step 7: User Feedback and Feature Enhancements

Encourage users to provide feedback on the AI writing tool's performance and features. Use this feedback to prioritize and implement new features or improvements that align with user needs and expectations.

Step 8: Security Audits

Perform regular security audits to identify and address potential vulnerabilities in the AI writing tool. Engage security experts to conduct penetration testing and security assessments to ensure the tool is resilient against cyber threats.

Step 9: Scalability Assessment

Regularly assess the scalability of the AI writing tool as the user base and data volume grow. Make necessary adjustments to accommodate increased demand and ensure optimal performance.

Step 10: Documentation Updates

Keep the documentation up to date to reflect changes and improvements made during the continuous monitoring and maintenance process. This includes updating user guides, developer documentation, and system architecture diagrams.

By following this continuous monitoring and maintenance approach, you can ensure that the AI writing tool remains robust, secure, and efficient throughout its lifecycle. Regularly assess its performance, address issues promptly, and keep the tool updated to meet user needs effectively.

By following the steps outlined above, you can effectively deploy your NLP AI tool for novel writing, ensuring scalability, efficiency, and security. Continuous monitoring and maintenance will help you keep the tool up-to-date and aligned with user expectations.

10. Intellectual Property Protection

If your tool is proprietary and you want to protect your intellectual property, consult legal experts to explore options for patents, copyrights, or other forms of intellectual property protection.

Intellectual property protection is an important consideration when developing a proprietary NLP AI tool for novel writing. It involves safeguarding your tool's intellectual property rights to ensure that your innovative ideas and creations are protected. Here's a detailed explanation of the steps involved:

Consult with Legal Experts

Seek advice from legal professionals specializing in intellectual property law. They can help you understand the available options for protecting your tool and guide you through the necessary legal processes.

Intellectual property protection is crucial when developing an AI writing tool using NLP techniques. In this section, we will discuss the importance of consulting with legal experts to ensure that the tool and its components are appropriately protected from any potential infringements or misuse. Consulting legal experts will help you navigate the complex landscape of intellectual property rights and implement the necessary measures to safeguard your work.

Understanding Intellectual Property Rights:

Familiarize yourself with the various forms of intellectual property protection, including patents, copyrights, trade secrets, trademarks, and more.

Gain insights into the scope and limitations of each form of protection and how they apply to the components of your AI writing tool.

Identifying Potential Intellectual Property:

Conduct a thorough review of your AI writing tool's components, including the language model, novel writing features, user interface, and any innovative algorithms or techniques you've developed.

Identify elements that may be eligible for intellectual property protection.

Seek Legal Expertise:

Look for qualified intellectual property attorneys or legal firms with experience in technology and AI-related matters.

Schedule consultations to discuss the specifics of your AI writing tool and seek advice on the appropriate protection mechanisms.

Patent Protection:

Discuss the possibility of patent protection for any novel algorithms or techniques used in your AI writing tool.

Work with legal experts to draft and file patent applications, adhering to the relevant patent laws and regulations.

Copyright Protection:

Understand the scope of copyright protection for your AI writing tool's code, user interface, and any original written content it generates.

Register copyrights for eligible components to strengthen your legal position in case of infringement.

Trade Secret Protection:

Evaluate whether certain aspects of your AI writing tool can be treated as trade secrets.

Work with legal experts to implement appropriate confidentiality measures to safeguard trade secrets from unauthorized disclosure.

Trademark Protection:

Discuss the possibility of trademarking your AI writing tool's name, logo, or any other distinctive branding elements.

File trademark applications and adhere to the required processes for securing trademarks.

Non-Disclosure Agreements (NDAs):

Consider using NDAs when sharing sensitive information about your AI writing tool with collaborators, stakeholders, or potential investors.

Draft clear and legally sound NDAs with the help of legal experts.

Documentation and Record-Keeping:

Maintain comprehensive documentation of all interactions with legal experts, including advice received and actions taken.

Keep records of patent filings, copyright registrations, trademark applications, and any other relevant legal documentation.

Monitoring and Enforcement:

Work with legal experts to establish monitoring mechanisms to identify potential infringements or violations of your AI writing tool's intellectual property rights.

Develop a strategy for enforcing your intellectual property rights and addressing any instances of infringement.

Remember that intellectual property laws and regulations can vary depending on your jurisdiction, so consulting with legal experts in the relevant regions is essential. By taking these steps and seeking professional legal advice, you can protect your AI writing tool and its innovations effectively.

Patent Protection

Explore the possibility of obtaining a patent for your tool. A patent provides exclusive rights to your invention, preventing others from making, using, or selling your novel NLP AI tool without your permission. Work closely with a patent attorney to assess the patentability of your tool and prepare the required documentation.

Patent protection is a crucial aspect of safeguarding the innovative aspects of your AI writing tool. In this section, we will explore the process of obtaining patent protection for the novel algorithms or techniques used in your tool. Please note that patent laws and procedures may vary based on the jurisdiction, so consulting with a qualified intellectual property attorney is highly recommended to ensure compliance with the relevant regulations.

Identify Patentable Components:

Review your AI writing tool's features, algorithms, or methods to identify unique and innovative aspects that may be eligible for patent protection.

Patentable components could include novel machine learning algorithms, language modeling techniques, or any other inventive solutions that contribute to the tool's functionality.

Prior Art Search:

Conduct a comprehensive prior art search to determine if similar patents or existing technologies already cover the aspects you wish to patent.

The prior art search is crucial to assess the novelty and non-obviousness of your invention, which are essential criteria for patentability.

Engage with a Patent Attorney:

Find a reputable patent attorney or patent law firm experienced in AI and NLP technologies.

Schedule a consultation to discuss your AI writing tool and explore the potential for patent protection.

Drafting the Patent Application:

Work closely with your patent attorney to draft a detailed and accurate patent application.

The application should describe the invention's technical details, its unique features, and its potential applications in the field of AI writing.

Filing the Patent Application:

Once the patent application is complete, your attorney will file it with the appropriate patent office, such as the United States Patent and Trademark Office (USPTO) in the USA or the European Patent Office (EPO) in Europe.

Pay the necessary filing fees and comply with all the formalities required by the patent office.

Patent Examination:

After filing, the patent office will conduct a thorough examination of your application.

This examination process may involve reviewing prior art, assessing the patent's novelty and non-obviousness, and evaluating its industrial applicability.

Responding to Office Actions:

If the patent office raises any objections or issues during the examination, work with your patent attorney to prepare and submit responses to address these concerns.

Amendments or clarifications may be necessary to overcome potential rejections.

Grant of Patent:

If the patent office determines that your AI writing tool invention meets all patentability requirements, they will grant the patent.

The patent grant provides you with exclusive rights to the patented invention for a limited period (usually 20 years from the filing date).

International Considerations:

Consider filing for international patent protection in countries where you plan to market or use your AI writing tool.

Work with your patent attorney to navigate the complexities of international patent filings and ensure compliance with each country's requirements.

Enforcement and Maintenance:

Once the patent is granted, it is your responsibility to enforce the patent rights and protect your invention from unauthorized use.

Additionally, be aware of the maintenance fees and requirements to keep the patent in force throughout its validity period.

Remember that obtaining a patent can be a complex and time-consuming process. Seek the guidance of a skilled patent attorney to maximize the chances of obtaining meaningful patent protection for your AI writing tool's innovative features.

Copyright Protection

Consider applying for copyright protection for your tool's software code, user interface designs, and any other creative elements that can be considered original works of authorship. Copyright protection grants you the exclusive right to reproduce, distribute, and modify your creative works.

Copyright protection is essential for safeguarding the original creative expression of your AI writing tool, such as the code, user interface, documentation, and other written materials. In this section, we will explore the process of obtaining and managing copyright protection for your AI writing tool. Please note that copyright laws may vary based on the jurisdiction, so it's advisable to consult with a qualified intellectual property attorney to ensure compliance with the relevant regulations.

Identify Copyrightable Works:

Make a comprehensive list of all the copyrightable elements in your AI writing tool. This may include the source code, user interface design, user guides, training materials, and any other written content.

Understand Copyright Duration and Requirements:

Familiarize yourself with the copyright duration in your country. In many jurisdictions, copyright protection extends for the lifetime of the creator plus a certain number of years after their death.

Unlike patents, copyright protection is granted automatically upon the creation of an original work; however, registering the copyright provides additional benefits.

Register Copyright (Optional but Recommended):

While copyright protection is granted automatically, registering your copyright with the appropriate copyright office provides additional legal advantages, including the ability to sue for statutory damages and attorney's fees in case of infringement.

Determine the appropriate copyright office for your jurisdiction. For example, in the United States, you can register copyrights with the U.S. Copyright Office.

Preparing Copyright Registration:

Gather all the necessary materials for copyright registration, which may include the source code, design documents, written content, and other materials.

Prepare a complete and accurate application for copyright registration, including all required forms and filing fees.

Submitting Copyright Application:

File the copyright application with the relevant copyright office. If you are filing online, follow the specific guidelines and procedures provided by the copyright office.

Copyright Notice:

Display a copyright notice on your AI writing tool's website, user interface, and other relevant materials.

The copyright notice typically includes the copyright symbol (©), the year of first publication, and the name of the copyright owner (e.g., "Copyright © 2023, Your Name").

Copyright Management:

Keep a record of all copyrighted materials and their registration details for proper management and enforcement.

Implement internal policies to ensure that employees or collaborators are aware of copyright protection and respect copyright ownership.

Monitor for Infringement:

Regularly monitor online platforms and other channels for potential copyright infringement of your AI writing tool's materials.

If you discover any instances of unauthorized use, consult with your intellectual property attorney to take appropriate legal action.

License and Distribution:

Decide on the licensing terms for your AI writing tool. Determine whether you want to offer it under an open-source license, a commercial license, or a combination of both.

Clearly communicate the licensing terms to users and provide a copy of the license agreement when distributing the tool.

Remember that copyright protection applies to the original expression of ideas and not to the ideas themselves. For any specific legal advice related to copyright protection, consult with an intellectual property attorney familiar with the laws of your jurisdiction.

Trade Secret Protection

Evaluate whether certain aspects of your tool, such as proprietary algorithms or specific implementation details, can be kept as trade secrets. Trade secrets are valuable and confidential information that provides a competitive advantage. Take measures to maintain secrecy, such as implementing access controls, non-disclosure agreements, and limiting internal access to sensitive information.

Trade secret protection is essential for preserving the confidentiality of proprietary information and algorithms used in your AI writing tool. In this section, we will explore the process of identifying and protecting trade secrets to prevent unauthorized use or disclosure. Please note that trade secret laws may vary based on the jurisdiction, so it's advisable to consult with a qualified intellectual property attorney to ensure compliance with the relevant regulations.

Identify Trade Secrets:

Make a comprehensive list of all the elements of your AI writing tool that qualify as trade secrets. Trade secrets may include unique algorithms, data preprocessing methods, proprietary training techniques, or any other confidential information that gives your tool a competitive advantage.

Non-Disclosure Agreements (NDAs):

Implement non-disclosure agreements (NDAs) with all employees, collaborators, contractors, and anyone who has access to the trade secrets. NDAs legally bind these individuals to maintain the confidentiality of the trade secret information.

Limit Access to Trade Secrets:

Restrict access to trade secrets on a need-to-know basis. Only grant access to individuals who require it for their specific tasks and responsibilities.

Physical and Digital Security:

Ensure that physical access to trade secret documents or materials is limited and secure. Use locked cabinets, restricted areas, or other physical security measures as needed.

For digital security, employ access controls, encryption, and secure login credentials to prevent unauthorized access to digital trade secret repositories.

Employee Training:

Train all employees and team members on the importance of trade secret protection and the proper handling of confidential information. Ensure they understand their obligations under the NDA.

Document Trade Secrets:

Maintain clear documentation of each trade secret, including its specific nature, how it is used, and its significance in the AI writing tool's functionality.

Regular Assessments:

Conduct regular assessments of your AI writing tool and its trade secrets to identify any potential vulnerabilities or areas that require additional protection.

Implement Internal Controls:

Establish internal controls and procedures to monitor access to trade secrets and detect any unauthorized attempts to access or disclose them.

Vendor and Partner Agreements:

If you collaborate with vendors or partners, ensure that appropriate contractual agreements are in place to protect your trade secrets when sharing information with them.

Responding to Misappropriation:

In case of suspected trade secret misappropriation, promptly investigate the matter and take necessary legal actions, if needed, to enforce your trade secret rights.

Regular Review of Trade Secrets:

Periodically review the list of trade secrets to ensure they remain relevant and valuable to your AI writing tool. Remove any information that no longer qualifies as a trade secret.

Remember that trade secret protection requires ongoing vigilance and maintenance. It is crucial to establish a company culture that values and prioritizes the protection of confidential information. For any specific legal advice related to trade secret protection, consult with an intellectual property attorney familiar with the laws of your jurisdiction.

Non-Disclosure Agreements

Use non-disclosure agreements (NDAs) when sharing confidential information about your NLP AI tool with collaborators, employees, or potential partners. NDAs ensure that the receiving party understands their obligation to maintain the confidentiality of the disclosed information.

Non-Disclosure Agreements (NDAs) play a crucial role in protecting your intellectual property and sensitive information when collaborating with team members, contractors, partners, or any other external entities. In this section, we'll delve into the process of creating and implementing effective NDAs to safeguard your AI writing tool's proprietary knowledge. Please remember that legal requirements for NDAs can vary by jurisdiction, so consult with an intellectual property attorney to ensure your NDAs are enforceable in your region.

Identify Confidential Information:

Make a comprehensive list of all the information you consider confidential. This includes trade secrets, proprietary algorithms, training data, unique methodologies, and any other sensitive information related to your AI writing tool.

NDA Template:

Create a standard NDA template that can be customized based on the specific nature of the collaboration. You may seek legal assistance to draft a robust NDA template that complies with relevant laws and adequately protects your interests.

Customize the NDA:

For each collaboration, review the NDA template and tailor it to suit the specific parties involved, the scope of the collaboration, and the information being shared.

Consult with Legal Experts:

Before sharing the NDA with any party, consult with legal experts to ensure its compliance with local laws and that it covers all the necessary elements to protect your intellectual property.

Provide Clear Explanations:

When sharing the NDA with collaborators or contractors, provide clear explanations of the purpose and importance of the NDA. Emphasize the need to keep the information confidential.

Execution and Signatures:

Ensure that all parties involved in the collaboration sign the NDA before any sensitive information is shared. Electronic signatures are legally valid in many jurisdictions, but verify the requirements in your region.

Retain Copies:

Maintain copies of signed NDAs for your records. This documentation will be crucial in case of any disputes or alleged breaches.

NDA Duration:

Specify the duration for which the NDA remains valid. The duration should be reasonable and relevant to the nature of the information being shared.

Restrictions and Permitted Uses:

Clearly outline what actions are prohibited under the NDA, such as unauthorized disclosure, reproduction, or use of the confidential information.

Also, specify any permitted uses of the information, such as using it solely for the purpose of the collaboration.

Consequences of Breach:

Clearly define the consequences of breaching the NDA. This may include legal action, financial penalties, or other remedies available under the law.

NDA Review:

Periodically review your NDA template to ensure it remains up-to-date with any changes in the law or business practices.

It's important to remember that NDAs are legally binding agreements, and any breach can have serious consequences. Take the time to create strong NDAs and ensure that all parties involved understand and adhere to their terms. Additionally, maintaining a culture of confidentiality and trust within your team is crucial for successful protection of your intellectual property.

Trademark Protection

Consider protecting your tool's brand identity through trademark registration. A registered trademark provides legal protection for your tool's name, logo, or other identifying marks. It helps prevent others from using similar marks that could cause confusion among users.

Trademarks are essential for protecting the brand identity and reputation of your AI writing tool. A trademark can be a name, logo, slogan, or any distinctive symbol that identifies and distinguishes your product from others in the market. In this section, we'll explore the process of registering and enforcing trademarks to safeguard your intellectual property rights.

Conduct a Trademark Search:

Before filing a trademark application, conduct a thorough search to ensure that your desired trademark is not already in use by another company or entity. Use the United States Patent and Trademark Office (USPTO) or similar databases in your country to perform the search.

Trademark Classes and Categories:

Familiarize yourself with the different classes and categories of trademarks to understand which class your AI writing tool falls under. Classify your trademark appropriately, as each class corresponds to specific goods or services.

Prepare the Trademark Application:

Prepare the necessary documents for the trademark application, which may include the application form, a clear representation of the trademark, a description of the goods/services associated with the trademark, and the filing fee.

File the Trademark Application:

Submit the completed trademark application to the appropriate government agency responsible for trademark registration. In the United States, this is the USPTO.

Trademark Examination:

The trademark application will undergo an examination process by the trademark office. They will review the application to ensure it meets all the legal requirements for registration.

Response to Office Actions (if applicable):

If the trademark office issues any objections or requests for clarification (known as "office actions"), respond promptly and adequately to address the issues raised.

Trademark Publication:

If the application is approved, the trademark will be published in an official gazette or journal, allowing third parties to oppose the registration if they believe it infringes on their existing rights.

Trademark Registration:

If there are no oppositions or if any oppositions are successfully resolved, your trademark will be registered. You will receive a registration certificate, granting you exclusive rights to use the trademark in association with the registered goods/services.

Monitor and Enforce the Trademark:

After registration, actively monitor the use of your trademark to identify any potential infringements. Enforce your trademark rights by taking legal action against unauthorized use.

Trademark Renewal:

Trademarks require periodic renewal to maintain their protection. In many countries, trademarks must be renewed every 10 years. Stay vigilant and ensure timely renewals to keep your trademark active.

Trademark Usage Guidelines:

Establish guidelines for the proper and consistent use of your trademark. This ensures that it maintains its distinctiveness and avoids becoming a generic term.

Educate Team Members and Partners:

Educate your team members, partners, and collaborators about the proper use of the trademark and the importance of maintaining its integrity.

Remember that the trademark application process can be complex, and it is advisable to seek legal advice from a trademark attorney to guide you through the process. Additionally, consider international trademark protection if you plan to offer your AI writing tool in multiple countries, as trademark protection is territorial and must be sought in each relevant jurisdiction.

Documentation and Record-Keeping

Maintain thorough documentation of the development process, including design documents, research notes, and invention disclosure records. These documents can be valuable evidence to support your intellectual property claims and establish your ownership rights.

Proper documentation and record-keeping are crucial for maintaining and protecting your intellectual property rights. In this section, we will outline the steps to create comprehensive documentation and establish a systematic approach to record-keeping for your AI writing tool.

Establish an Intellectual Property Policy:

Start by developing an intellectual property policy that outlines the types of intellectual property assets associated with your AI writing tool, including trademarks, copyrights, patents, trade secrets, and any other proprietary information.

Document Creation and Ownership:

Clearly define the process for creating new intellectual property assets within your organization. This includes guidelines for employee contributions, third-party collaborations, and individual contributions.

Copyright Notice:

For written content, software code, or any other creative work associated with your AI writing tool, add a copyright notice to indicate ownership and the year of creation. The notice should follow the format "Copyright © [Year] [Your Company/Organization Name]. All rights reserved."

Patent Documentation:

If applicable, document the invention disclosure process for potential patentable features of your AI writing tool. Work with legal experts to assess the patentability of the technology and proceed with filing a patent application if necessary.

Trade Secret Protection:

Identify any trade secrets that contribute to the unique functionality or competitive advantage of your AI writing tool. Implement measures to keep this information confidential, such as non-disclosure agreements (NDAs) with employees and collaborators.

Trademark Registration Documentation:

Maintain detailed records of the trademark registration process, including the search reports, application forms, representations of the trademark, and correspondence with the trademark office.

Document Version Control:

Implement a version control system for all intellectual property documents. This ensures that you can track changes, updates, and revisions to the documentation over time.

Intellectual Property Assignments:

When employees or contractors contribute to the development of your AI writing tool, require them to sign intellectual property assignment agreements. These agreements transfer the ownership of their contributions to your organization.

Confidentiality Agreements:

If your AI writing tool involves collaborations with external parties, such as vendors or partners, use confidentiality agreements to protect sensitive information shared during the collaboration.

Record Maintenance:

Regularly update and maintain your intellectual property records. Ensure that all documentation is stored securely and backed up to prevent loss or unauthorized access.

Monitoring and Enforcement:

Implement a monitoring and enforcement system to identify and address any potential infringement of your intellectual property rights. Take prompt action to protect your assets if any violations are detected.

Educate Your Team:

Educate your team members about the importance of intellectual property protection and the procedures for documentation and record-keeping. Foster a culture of awareness and respect for intellectual property rights.

Remember that intellectual property laws may vary depending on your country or region. To ensure the best protection for your AI writing tool, consult with legal experts who specialize in intellectual property law and keep yourself updated on any changes in regulations.

Monitoring and Enforcement

Regularly monitor the market to detect any potential infringement of your intellectual property rights. Stay informed about similar tools or technologies being introduced and take appropriate action if you believe your rights are being violated. Consult with legal experts to enforce your rights and protect your tool's intellectual property.

Once you have established intellectual property protection measures for your AI writing tool, it's essential to implement monitoring and enforcement strategies to safeguard your rights. This section outlines the steps to monitor and enforce your intellectual property.

Intellectual Property Auditing:

Conduct regular intellectual property audits to assess the status of your protected assets. This involves reviewing your patents, trademarks, copyrights, trade secrets, and any other protected information.

Track Expiration Dates:

Keep track of the expiration dates of your patents and trademarks. Some intellectual property rights have limited durations, and it's crucial to know when they will expire.

Monitor for Infringements:

Utilize various tools and services to monitor the use of your AI writing tool's intellectual property. Look for instances of unauthorized use or infringement.

Online Monitoring:

Implement online monitoring to track potential unauthorized use of your AI writing tool's content, software, or trademarks on websites, social media platforms, and other digital spaces.

Patent and Trademark Watch Services:

Enlist the help of professional patent and trademark watch services to receive alerts about potential infringements or unauthorized use of your protected assets.

Infringement Notification:

If you discover instances of infringement, send cease and desist letters or infringement notifications to the involved parties. Clearly state your intellectual property rights and the actions required to resolve the issue.

Legal Action:

Consult with legal experts to determine whether legal action is necessary to enforce your intellectual property rights. This could include filing lawsuits, seeking injunctions, or taking other legal measures to protect your assets.

Takedown Notices:

For online infringement, issue takedown notices to relevant platforms or hosting providers in accordance with the Digital Millennium Copyright Act (DMCA) or similar laws in your jurisdiction.

International Enforcement:

If your AI writing tool operates globally, consider international enforcement of your intellectual property rights. Work with legal experts who have expertise in international intellectual property laws and regulations.

Settlement and Licensing:

In some cases, it may be beneficial to explore settlement or licensing agreements with parties engaged in unauthorized use. This could result in compensation for the use of your intellectual property.

Monitor Industry Trends:

Stay informed about industry trends and technological developments to proactively protect your intellectual property against emerging threats or potential infringements.

Educate Your Team:

Ensure that your team members are aware of the importance of monitoring and enforcing intellectual property rights. Encourage them to report any potential infringements they come across.

Remember that intellectual property enforcement can be a complex and time-consuming process. Seek legal advice and guidance to ensure that your actions are in compliance with applicable laws and regulations. Additionally, continuous monitoring and enforcement efforts will help safeguard your AI writing tool's intellectual property over time.

International Considerations

If you plan to market your tool globally, consider international intellectual property protection. Research and understand the intellectual property laws and regulations of the countries in which you intend to operate or sell your tool. Consult with legal experts who specialize in international intellectual property to navigate the complexities of international protection.

Protecting your AI writing tool's intellectual property internationally requires careful consideration and adherence to the laws and regulations of different jurisdictions. This section outlines the steps and considerations for international intellectual property protection.

Identify Target Markets:

Determine the countries or regions where you plan to offer your AI writing tool. These are the jurisdictions where you need to seek intellectual property protection.

Research International IP Laws:

Conduct thorough research on the intellectual property laws of each target market. Understand the differences in patent, trademark, and copyright laws, as well as any specific requirements or procedures for registration and enforcement.

Seek Legal Assistance:

Engage legal experts with expertise in international intellectual property laws. They can guide you through the complexities of different jurisdictions and help you develop a comprehensive strategy.

File International Patents:

If your AI writing tool includes novel inventions or processes, consider filing international patents under the Patent Cooperation Treaty (PCT). The PCT allows you to seek patent protection in multiple countries through a single application.

Register International Trademarks:

Register your trademarks in each target country to protect your brand identity. Some countries follow a "first-to-file" system, so early registration is crucial to prevent trademark squatting.

International Copyright Protection:

Copyright protection is generally automatic in many countries through the Berne Convention. However, consider registering your copyrights with relevant authorities in certain countries to strengthen enforcement options.

Understand Regional Treaties and Agreements:

Familiarize yourself with regional treaties and agreements that facilitate intellectual property protection, such as the European Union Intellectual Property Office (EUIPO) or the African Regional Intellectual Property Organization (ARIPO).

Translation and Localization:

Ensure that all intellectual property documentation, including patents, trademarks, and copyrights, are translated accurately into the official languages of the target countries. This ensures that your rights are well-understood and enforceable.

Monitor International Infringements:

Implement a robust system to monitor and detect potential infringements in different jurisdictions. Consider employing local intellectual property agents or investigators to identify unauthorized use.

Enforce Intellectual Property Rights:

Be prepared to take appropriate legal action in each country where you encounter intellectual property infringements. This may involve filing lawsuits, sending cease and desist letters, or pursuing alternative dispute resolution methods.

Be Mindful of Cultural Differences:

Respect cultural sensitivities and legal practices in each jurisdiction. Adapt your intellectual property protection strategies to align with local customs and norms.

Stay Updated on Changes:

Intellectual property laws can evolve over time. Stay updated on changes in international IP laws and regulations to ensure ongoing compliance and protection.

Remember that international intellectual property protection can be complex and costly. Allocate sufficient resources and plan strategically to maximize the effectiveness of your efforts in safeguarding your AI writing tool's intellectual property worldwide.

Ongoing Review and Maintenance

Intellectual property protection is an ongoing process. Regularly review and update your intellectual property strategy as your tool evolves and new features are added. Stay informed about changes in intellectual property laws and regulations that may affect your rights or present new opportunities for protection.

Once you have implemented intellectual property protection measures for your AI writing tool, it is crucial to maintain and review these safeguards continuously. This section outlines the steps to ensure ongoing review and maintenance of intellectual property.

Regular IP Audits:

Conduct periodic intellectual property audits to assess the effectiveness of your protection measures. An IP audit involves reviewing your patents, trademarks, copyrights, and trade secrets to identify any potential weaknesses or areas for improvement.

Monitoring New Technologies and Innovations:

Stay updated on the latest advancements in AI, NLP, and related technologies. Monitor industry trends to ensure your AI writing tool remains innovative and competitive, while also evaluating if any new features or technologies require additional intellectual property protection.

Evaluate Changes in Laws and Regulations:

Intellectual property laws and regulations may evolve over time. Stay informed about changes in the legal landscape, both domestically and internationally, that could impact your existing protections or require new measures.

Periodic Consultation with Legal Experts:

Regularly consult with legal experts specializing in intellectual property. Seek their guidance on updates to your protection strategies and any necessary adjustments based on changing circumstances.

Documentation and Record-Keeping:

Maintain accurate and up-to-date documentation related to your intellectual property, including registration certificates, licenses, and agreements. Proper record-keeping helps with enforcement efforts and disputes, if any arise.

Educate and Train Employees:

Ensure that your team, especially those involved in AI development and intellectual property management, receive regular training on the importance of IP protection and the proper handling of sensitive information.

Monitor and Address Potential Infringements:

Implement an ongoing monitoring system to detect potential intellectual property infringements. Be prepared to take swift and appropriate action against any unauthorized use or violations.

Continuously Improve Security Measures:

Regularly assess the security measures in place to safeguard your AI writing tool's proprietary data and code. Implement improvements as needed to prevent unauthorized access or data breaches.

Review Licensing and Non-Disclosure Agreements:

Reevaluate licensing and non-disclosure agreements with third parties to ensure they align with your current intellectual property protection needs and provide adequate safeguards.

Collaborate with Industry Associations:

Engage with relevant industry associations or consortiums focused on AI and NLP. Collaborating with peers can help you stay informed about best practices and emerging threats in the industry.

Monitor and Address International Considerations:

Stay vigilant about changes in international intellectual property laws and regulations. Monitor your AI writing tool's use and distribution in different countries to ensure compliance with each jurisdiction's requirements.

Implement a Continuous Improvement Process:

Establish a systematic process for ongoing review and improvement of your intellectual property protection strategies. Regularly update and refine your approaches based on feedback, experience, and changes in the AI landscape.

Remember that intellectual property protection is not a one-time task; it requires ongoing effort and vigilance. By maintaining a proactive approach and continuously reviewing and improving your strategies, you can better safeguard the valuable assets associated with your AI writing tool.

Remember that intellectual property protection is a complex area of law, and it is crucial to consult with legal professionals who specialize in intellectual property to ensure that your tool's intellectual property rights are adequately protected.

It's important to note that the information provided here is general in nature and does not constitute legal advice. Seek guidance from legal professionals to tailor the intellectual property protection strategy to your specific circumstances and jurisdiction.

11.

Collaboration and Expertise

Welcome to the appendices section of this comprehensive guide! In this section, you'll find additional resources, references, and supplementary information to further enhance your understanding of data mining with Python. The appendices serve as a valuable reference point, offering you practical tools, code snippets, and in-depth explanations to support your data mining journey. Whether you're seeking additional code examples, want to explore advanced topics, or need guidance on specific techniques, the appendices have got you covered. So, let's dive in and expand your knowledge even further!

Developing an advanced NLP AI tool for novel writing requires significant expertise in machine learning, natural language processing, and software development. Collaborating with a team of experts or hiring professionals can help you bridge any knowledge gaps and ensure the successful development and implementation of your tool. Here's a detailed explanation of the steps involved:

Identify Skill Gaps

Assess your own skills and expertise in machine learning, natural language processing, and software development. Identify areas where you may need additional support or specialized knowledge. Determine the specific roles and skills required to build and deploy your NLP AI tool effectively.

Identifying skill gaps within your team is a crucial step in successfully crafting an AI-powered novel writing tool. This process helps you understand what expertise is needed to fill those gaps, ensuring that you have a well-rounded and capable team to tackle the challenges of the project. Here's a step-by-step guide on how to identify skill gaps:

Conduct a Skills Assessment:

Evaluate the current skills and expertise of each team member involved in the AI writing tool development. This assessment should cover areas such as NLP, machine learning, software development, user interface design, project management, and domain knowledge related to novel writing.

Define Project Requirements:

Clearly outline the requirements of your AI writing tool project. Consider the scope, complexity, and desired features of the tool. These requirements will help you determine the specific skills needed for successful project execution.

Identify Critical Areas:

Based on the project requirements, identify critical areas that require specialized knowledge or experience. For example, natural language processing (NLP) expertise might be crucial for developing the language model, while user interface design skills are essential for creating an intuitive writing interface.

Analyze Existing Skill Sets:

Compare the current skills of your team members to the identified critical areas. Determine if there are any skill gaps that need to be addressed. Note down the specific skills that are lacking or underrepresented in the team.

Prioritize Skill Gaps:

Prioritize the identified skill gaps based on their significance to the project's success. Some gaps may be more critical and urgent to address than others.

Define Desired Skill Set for Each Role:

Clearly outline the desired skill set for each role in the team. This will help you set clear expectations for hiring new team members or upskilling existing ones.

Consider Cross-Training and Upskilling:

Explore the possibility of cross-training or upskilling existing team members to fill certain skill gaps. This approach can be more cost-effective and also boosts team morale.

Recruit New Talent:

If there are skill gaps that cannot be filled through internal resources, consider recruiting new talent with the required expertise. Advertise job openings and conduct interviews to find suitable candidates.

Collaborate with External Experts:

If hiring is not feasible, consider collaborating with external experts or consultants who can provide the necessary skills on a temporary basis.

Training and Development:

Invest in continuous training and development programs to enhance the skills of your team members. Provide opportunities for them to learn new technologies and stay updated on industry trends.

Foster a Learning Culture:

Encourage a learning culture within the team, where team members are motivated to expand their knowledge and share their expertise with others.

By following these steps, you can systematically identify skill gaps within your team and take appropriate actions to ensure that you have the right expertise to successfully craft and maintain the AI-powered novel writing tool. A well-rounded team with diverse skills and knowledge will significantly contribute to the success of your project.

Build a Team

Assemble a team of experts with complementary skills and knowledge. This can include machine learning engineers, NLP specialists, software developers, data scientists, user experience designers, and project managers. Consider collaborating with individuals who have experience in developing NLP AI tools or working on similar projects.

Building a capable and efficient team is vital to the success of your AI-powered novel writing project. A well-structured team with diverse expertise will ensure that all aspects of the project are addressed effectively. Here's a step-by-step guide on how to build a team for your NLP-based novel writing AI project:

Identify Project Requirements:

Understand the scope and objectives of your AI project. Analyze the key features and functionalities that the novel writing tool will offer. Determine the necessary skills and roles required to accomplish these objectives.

Define Team Roles:

Based on the project requirements, define the various roles that need to be filled. Common roles for an AI project include NLP experts, machine learning engineers, software developers, user interface designers, project managers, and domain experts in novel writing.

Create Job Descriptions:

Prepare clear and detailed job descriptions for each role. Specify the qualifications, skills, and experience needed for each position. These job descriptions will guide you in finding suitable candidates.

Internal Resources:

Assess your existing team members to identify if any of them possess the skills required for the project. Consider providing opportunities for upskilling or cross-training to fill any skill gaps internally.

External Recruitment:

If there are skill gaps that cannot be filled internally, start the external recruitment process. Advertise job openings on relevant platforms and job boards, and use your professional network to reach potential candidates.

Consider Freelancers or Consultants:

For specific tasks or short-term needs, consider hiring freelancers or consultants with specialized expertise. This can be a cost-effective way to access skills that may not be needed full-time.

Evaluate Candidates:

Conduct thorough interviews and assessments to evaluate candidates' technical skills, experience, and compatibility with the team. Consider both technical proficiency and collaborative qualities.

Foster Diversity and Inclusion:

Aim to build a diverse team with individuals from different backgrounds and experiences. Diversity can bring fresh perspectives and creativity to the project.

Communication and Collaboration:

Ensure that team members can communicate effectively and collaborate seamlessly. Encourage an open and supportive work environment where ideas and feedback are valued.

Team Dynamics:

Pay attention to team dynamics and encourage healthy working relationships among team members. Foster a positive and motivated atmosphere to boost productivity.

Continuous Learning:

Promote a culture of continuous learning and improvement. Encourage team members to stay updated with the latest advancements in NLP and machine learning.

Establish Clear Goals and Expectations:

Clearly communicate the project goals, expectations, and timelines to the team. Ensure that everyone understands their roles and responsibilities.

Building a skilled and collaborative team is a crucial step in successfully harnessing the power of NLP for novel writing. A well-functioning team will be able to efficiently execute the different stages of the project, from data collection and model training to user interface design and deployment. Regularly review team performance and provide support and resources as needed to achieve the best possible outcome.

Define Roles and Responsibilities

Clearly define the roles and responsibilities of each team member. Assign tasks and establish clear communication channels to ensure efficient collaboration. Encourage open discussions and idea sharing to leverage the collective expertise of the team.

In order to foster a collaborative and efficient team, it is essential to clearly define the roles and responsibilities of each team member in the AI-powered novel writing project. This section outlines the steps to define roles and responsibilities effectively:

Identify Project Requirements:

Review the project scope, goals, and objectives to understand the specific needs and tasks required for successful implementation. Identify the key areas that need expertise and contribution.

List Key Roles:

Based on the project requirements, create a list of key roles necessary for the project. Common roles may include NLP experts, machine learning engineers, software developers, user interface designers, project managers, domain experts in novel writing, and quality assurance specialists.

Define Role Descriptions:

Prepare detailed role descriptions for each position. Clearly outline the primary responsibilities, required skills, qualifications, and experience for each role. Specify the expected contributions to the project.

Identify Skill Sets:

Determine the specific skill sets required for each role. Consider technical proficiency in NLP, machine learning, programming languages, user interface design, project management, and other relevant domains.

Cross-functional Collaboration:

Ensure that roles are defined in a way that promotes cross-functional collaboration. Identify areas of overlap between roles and establish clear communication channels for effective coordination.

Establish Reporting Structure:

Define the reporting structure within the team. Determine the hierarchy, if any, and establish lines of communication for feedback, updates, and reporting progress.

Collaborative Decision-making:

Encourage collaborative decision-making within the team. Clearly communicate that each team member's input is valued and that decisions are made collectively when appropriate.

Create Role Alignment:

Ensure that each team member understands how their role aligns with the overall project objectives. This alignment will foster a sense of purpose and ownership among team members.

Allocate Responsibilities:

Assign specific responsibilities to each team member based on their expertise and role descriptions. Ensure that these responsibilities align with the project timeline and goals.

Clarify Expectations:

Clearly communicate the expectations for each role, including deadlines, quality standards, and any other relevant performance indicators.

Training and Support:

If team members lack certain skills or experience, provide training and support to help them excel in their roles. Encourage continuous learning and improvement.

Regularly Review Roles:

Periodically review the roles and responsibilities as the project progresses. Be open to adjusting roles based on changing project needs or team dynamics.

Defining roles and responsibilities is crucial for effective project management and team collaboration. A well-defined team structure will ensure that each team member knows their contributions and how they fit into the bigger picture. This clarity will lead to improved efficiency, communication, and overall project success.

Collaborate on Design and Development

Work collaboratively with the team to define the tool's architecture, algorithms, and implementation strategies. Leverage the expertise of your team members to make informed decisions and incorporate best practices. Regularly review progress, provide feedback, and address any challenges that arise during the development process.

Collaboration is a key factor in the success of an AI-powered novel writing project. This section outlines the steps to foster effective collaboration during the design and development phase:

Conduct Regular Team Meetings:

Schedule regular team meetings to discuss progress, updates, and challenges. Use these meetings to brainstorm ideas, share insights, and make collective decisions.

Use Collaborative Tools:

Utilize collaborative tools such as project management software, version control systems, and communication platforms to streamline teamwork and keep everyone on the same page.

Establish Clear Communication Channels:

Define clear communication channels for different aspects of the project. Use instant messaging, email, or project management tools for day-to-day communication, and schedule formal meetings for critical discussions.

Foster an Open and Inclusive Environment:

Create a culture of openness and inclusivity where team members feel comfortable sharing their ideas and opinions. Encourage constructive feedback and welcome diverse perspectives.

Promote Knowledge Sharing:

Encourage team members to share their knowledge and expertise with others. Organize knowledge-sharing sessions or workshops to facilitate cross-functional learning.

Cross-Functional Collaboration:

Facilitate cross-functional collaboration by encouraging team members from different areas (e.g., NLP experts, developers, writers) to work together on specific tasks or features.

Define Design Guidelines:

Establish design guidelines and standards to ensure consistency in the user interface and user experience. This will help create a coherent and polished product.

Implement Agile Methodology:

Consider adopting an agile development methodology to promote iterative and incremental progress. Agile practices like sprints and retrospectives enhance collaboration and adaptability.

Encourage Rapid Prototyping:

Encourage team members to create rapid prototypes of novel writing features. This allows for quick validation of ideas and facilitates continuous improvement.

Conduct Design Reviews:

Organize design reviews where team members present their ideas and designs to the rest of the team. Feedback from peers can lead to improvements and innovative solutions.

Use Design Thinking Techniques:

Apply design thinking techniques to explore user needs and generate creative solutions. Techniques like empathy mapping and user journey mapping can provide valuable insights.

Maintain Documentation:

Ensure that all design decisions and changes are documented for future reference. This documentation aids in knowledge sharing and understanding the project's evolution.

Resolve Conflicts Promptly:

Address conflicts and disagreements within the team promptly and constructively. A positive approach to conflict resolution strengthens collaboration and team dynamics.

By following these steps, the team can collaborate effectively during the design and development of the AI-powered novel writing system. Effective collaboration leads to a well-rounded and innovative product that meets user needs and achieves the project's goals and objectives.

Knowledge Sharing and Learning

Foster a culture of knowledge sharing within the team. Encourage team members to attend relevant conferences, workshops, or training programs to stay updated with the latest advancements in the field. Organize internal knowledge-sharing sessions to disseminate new insights and techniques among the team members.

In the development of an AI-powered novel writing system, fostering a culture of continuous learning and knowledge sharing is crucial for the success of the project. This section outlines the steps to promote knowledge sharing and learning within the team:

Conduct Learning Sessions:

Schedule regular learning sessions where team members can share their expertise, experiences, and insights related to NLP, machine learning, and novel writing. These sessions can take the form of workshops, seminars, or presentations.

Encourage Peer Learning:

Promote peer learning within the team. Encourage team members to pair up and work together on specific tasks, where one can learn from the other's expertise.

Organize Internal Workshops:

Organize internal workshops on specific topics relevant to the project. These workshops can be hands-on coding sessions, brainstorming exercises, or discussions on cutting-edge NLP techniques.

Share Research Papers and Resources:

Maintain a shared repository of research papers, articles, tutorials, and other relevant resources related to NLP, machine learning, and AI writing. Encourage team members to contribute to the repository.

Encourage Collaboration with External Experts:

Invite external experts in the field of NLP and AI to conduct workshops or provide talks to the team. These interactions can bring fresh perspectives and insights.

Allocate Time for Learning:

Dedicate a portion of the team's work schedule for learning and professional development. Allow team members to explore new techniques and tools related to their roles.

Set Up a Team Wiki or Documentation Platform:

Establish a team wiki or documentation platform to record and share knowledge within the team. Encourage team members to document their learnings and discoveries for future reference.

Promote Online Learning Platforms:

Encourage team members to enroll in online courses and certifications related to NLP, machine learning, and AI writing. Support their learning journey by providing resources and funding.

Conduct Hackathons and Challenges:

Organize hackathons or coding challenges related to novel AI writing. These events can spark creativity and innovation while providing opportunities for learning.

Implement Peer Code Reviews:

Encourage peer code reviews as part of the development process. This helps identify potential improvements and allows team members to learn from each other's code.

Attend Conferences and Webinars:

Sponsor team members to attend NLP, AI, and machine learning conferences, workshops, and webinars. These events offer exposure to the latest research and industry trends.

Recognize and Reward Learning Initiatives:

Recognize and reward team members who actively participate in knowledge sharing and learning initiatives. This fosters a culture of continuous improvement and motivation.

By following these steps, the team can create an environment that promotes knowledge sharing, continuous learning, and innovation. The collective expertise of the team will be enriched, leading to the development of a more advanced and sophisticated AI-powered novel writing system.

Continuous Communication

Establish regular communication channels to facilitate collaboration among team members. Schedule regular meetings, such as stand-ups or sprint reviews, to discuss progress, address issues, and align on project milestones. Use collaboration tools like project management software, version control systems, and communication platforms to streamline workflows and maintain transparency.

Effective communication is the backbone of any successful AI writing project. In this section, we will explore the strategies and practices to ensure continuous communication among team members, stakeholders, and users throughout the development process.

Set Up Regular Meetings:

Schedule regular team meetings to discuss progress, challenges, and updates on different aspects of the project. These meetings can be daily stand-ups or weekly status updates.

Use Collaboration Tools:

Utilize collaboration tools such as Slack, Microsoft Teams, or other project management platforms to facilitate real-time communication and quick exchange of ideas.

Maintain Communication Channels:

Set up dedicated communication channels for different project areas, such as a channel for NLP research, AI model development, UI/UX design, etc. This helps streamline discussions and keep information organized.

Conduct Virtual Meetings:

In addition to in-person meetings, conduct virtual meetings for team members who may be working remotely or are located in different time zones. Video conferencing tools can aid in face-to-face interactions.

Foster Open Discussions:

Encourage an open and inclusive communication culture where team members feel comfortable sharing their thoughts, ideas, and concerns without fear of judgment.

Document Meeting Minutes:

Assign a team member to document meeting minutes, action items, and decisions made during meetings. Share these minutes with all team members to ensure alignment and accountability.

Hold Brainstorming Sessions:

Organize brainstorming sessions to collectively tackle challenges and come up with innovative solutions. These sessions can spark creativity and cross-disciplinary collaboration.

Provide Feedback Loops:

Establish feedback loops between different teams and stakeholders. Encourage constructive feedback and consider it as a valuable source for improvement.

Conduct User Feedback Sessions:

Engage users in feedback sessions to understand their needs and pain points. This input is crucial for refining the AI-powered novel writing system.

Share Progress Updates:

Regularly share progress updates with stakeholders and end-users to keep them informed about the project's development and gather their feedback.

Address Issues Promptly:

Promptly address any issues, concerns, or roadblocks raised by team members, stakeholders, or users. Timely resolution is essential for maintaining project momentum.

Organize Knowledge Sharing Sessions:

Conduct knowledge sharing sessions to spread domain-specific knowledge across the team. These sessions can be led by subject matter experts within the team.

Maintain a Centralized Knowledge Base:

Create and maintain a centralized knowledge base or wiki that houses project-related information, design decisions, and best practices.

By implementing these strategies, the project team can ensure continuous communication, foster collaboration, and keep all stakeholders aligned throughout the development of the AI-powered novel writing system. Effective communication will enhance the team's ability to deliver a high-quality and successful product.

Quality Assurance

Implement rigorous quality assurance processes to ensure the effectiveness and reliability of your NLP AI tool. Conduct regular code reviews, testing, and debugging to identify and fix any issues or bugs. Utilize automated testing frameworks and validation techniques to validate the tool's performance against predefined criteria.

Quality assurance is a crucial aspect of developing an AI-powered novel writing system. In this section, we will explore the steps to ensure the quality of the system and its components before deployment.

Define Quality Metrics:

Clearly define the quality metrics that will be used to assess the performance of different modules within the AI writing system. These metrics could include accuracy, precision, recall, F1 score, perplexity, etc., depending on the specific components.

Create Test Cases:

Develop comprehensive test cases that cover different functionalities and scenarios of the system. Test cases should encompass various writing styles, genres, and language nuances.

Conduct Unit Testing:

Perform unit testing on individual components of the system, such as the grammar checking module, style suggestion module, etc. Use automated testing frameworks like pytest for efficient unit testing.

Perform Integration Testing:

Integrate different modules of the AI writing system and conduct integration testing to ensure smooth communication and functioning among the components.

Implement Regression Testing:

Implement regression testing to verify that new code changes or updates do not adversely affect the existing functionality of the system.

Conduct User Acceptance Testing (UAT):

Engage potential end-users or stakeholders to participate in user acceptance testing. Gather feedback and assess whether the system meets the defined requirements and objectives.

Validate Real-Time Suggestions:

Evaluate the real-time suggestion system using sample writing input from users. Verify that the suggestions provided by the AI model align with the desired writing style and tone.

Assess Usability:

Evaluate the user interface for usability and user experience. Consider factors such as ease of navigation, clarity of text input/output, and intuitiveness of features.

Check Performance and Scalability:

Assess the performance of the AI writing system under different loads to ensure it can handle concurrent user requests. Optimize code and infrastructure for scalability.

Address Bugs and Issues:

Track and address bugs or issues identified during testing promptly. Use issue tracking tools like Jira to manage bug resolution efficiently.

Review Documentation:

Ensure that all documentation, including user guides, installation guides, and technical documentation, is accurate, up-to-date, and easily accessible.

Conduct Code Reviews:

Perform code reviews to promote code quality, identify potential issues, and encourage best practices. Use code review tools such as GitHub pull requests for effective code collaboration.

Involve Quality Assurance Experts:

Consider involving quality assurance experts or external testers who can offer fresh perspectives and unbiased feedback on the system.

Continuous Improvement:

Continuously monitor user feedback and system performance after deployment. Use this feedback for continuous improvement of the AI writing system.

By rigorously following these quality assurance steps, the development team can ensure that the AI-powered novel writing system is robust, accurate, and meets the needs and expectations of its users. Quality assurance plays a vital role in delivering a reliable and high-quality AI writing tool.

Documentation and Knowledge Management

Document the development process, algorithms, methodologies, and implementation details. Maintain comprehensive documentation to facilitate knowledge transfer within the team and for future reference. Use version control systems to manage codebase revisions and track changes.

In the development process of the AI-powered novel writing system, proper documentation and knowledge management are essential to ensure seamless collaboration, facilitate understanding, and maintain the project's long-term success. This section will cover the steps to effectively manage documentation and knowledge.

Documentation Strategy:

Define a clear documentation strategy that outlines the types of documents to be created, their purpose, and the target audience. Common types of documentation include technical specifications, design documents, user guides, and API documentation.

Version Control for Documentation:

Use a version control system like Git to manage changes to documentation. This ensures that multiple team members can collaborate on documentation and track updates over time.

Centralized Documentation Repository:

Set up a centralized repository (e.g., GitHub repository, Confluence, or Google Drive) to store all project-related documentation. This ensures easy access and retrieval of documents.

API Documentation:

If your AI writing system exposes APIs for integration with other applications, create comprehensive API documentation. Use tools like Swagger/OpenAPI to generate API specifications automatically.

COLLABORATION AND EXPERTISE

User Guides:

Develop user guides to assist end-users in understanding how to use the AI writing system effectively. Include step-by-step instructions, examples, and troubleshooting tips.

Design and Architecture Documents:

Create design and architecture documents to provide an in-depth understanding of the system's structure and components. Include flowcharts, data flow diagrams, and system diagrams.

Knowledge Sharing Sessions:

Organize regular knowledge sharing sessions within the development team. Encourage team members to present and discuss their work to foster cross-functional learning.

Developer Onboarding Documentation:

Prepare detailed onboarding documents for new developers joining the project. These documents should cover the project's background, coding guidelines, and development environment setup.

Document Codebase:

Add inline comments and documentation within the codebase to explain complex algorithms, data structures, and functions. Use tools like Doxygen for automated code documentation.

Update Documentation Continuously:

Ensure that documentation is updated consistently as the project evolves. Require developers to update relevant documents whenever they make significant changes to the codebase.

Implement a Searchable Knowledge Base:

Set up a searchable knowledge base or wiki where team members can share insights, lessons learned, and best practices. Tools like Confluence or MediaWiki can be useful for this purpose.

Standardize Naming Conventions:

Standardize naming conventions for documents and files to make them easily identifiable. This improves organization and retrieval of information.

Backup and Data Recovery:

Regularly back up all project-related documentation to prevent data loss. Consider using cloud storage solutions and automated backup systems.

Create a Glossary:

Develop a glossary of technical terms and domain-specific jargon used in the project. This helps team members, stakeholders, and users have a shared understanding of the terminology.

By following these steps, the development team can establish effective documentation and knowledge management practices, promoting collaboration, efficiency, and continuous improvement throughout the development and maintenance of the AI writing system.

Project Management

Employ effective project management practices to ensure the successful execution of your NLP AI tool development. Define project milestones, establish timelines, and track progress against defined goals. Utilize project management methodologies such as Agile or Scrum to foster iterative and adaptive development.

Effective project management is crucial for the successful development and deployment of the AI-powered novel writing system. This section covers the key steps and best practices in project management to ensure that the project is completed on time, within budget, and meets the desired quality standards.

Define Project Objectives:

Clearly define the project objectives, including the target release date, key milestones, and success criteria. This will serve as a guiding framework throughout the project.

Project Scope and Work Breakdown:

Review and refine the defined scope of the project. Break down the project into manageable tasks and sub-tasks. Create a work breakdown structure (WBS) to organize and prioritize tasks.

Task Assignment:

Assign tasks to individual team members based on their expertise and availability. Ensure that each team member understands their responsibilities and deadlines.

Project Timeline:

Create a detailed project timeline with start and end dates for each task. Consider dependencies between tasks and buffer time for unforeseen delays.

Project Tracking and Communication:

Implement a project management tool (e.g., Trello, Jira, Asana) to track progress, monitor task completion, and manage communication among team members.

Risk Management:

Identify potential risks and challenges that may arise during the project. Develop a risk management plan to mitigate these risks and have contingency plans in place.

Agile Development:

Consider adopting an Agile development methodology to promote flexibility and adaptability in response to changing requirements and user feedback.

Regular Team Meetings:

Conduct regular team meetings to discuss progress, challenges, and updates. Use these meetings to address any roadblocks and make necessary adjustments to the project plan.

Stakeholder Communication:

Keep stakeholders informed about the project's progress through regular status updates, progress reports, and meetings.

Project Documentation:

Maintain comprehensive project documentation, including meeting minutes, project plans, progress reports, and change logs.

Continuous Integration and Deployment:

Implement continuous integration and deployment (CI/CD) practices to automate code integration, testing, and deployment processes. This ensures a smooth and consistent development workflow.

Quality Assurance:

Conduct thorough quality assurance testing at each development stage to identify and fix any bugs or issues. Use unit testing, integration testing, and user acceptance testing (UAT) for comprehensive testing.

User Acceptance Testing (UAT):

Involve end-users in the UAT process to gather feedback and ensure that the AI writing system meets their requirements and expectations.

Performance Monitoring:

Set up performance monitoring and logging to track system performance, identify bottlenecks, and optimize system efficiency.

Documentation and Knowledge Sharing:

Encourage knowledge sharing among team members by documenting best practices, lessons learned, and technical insights.

By implementing robust project management practices, the development team can effectively coordinate efforts, minimize risks, and deliver a high-quality AI-powered novel writing system within the planned timeline and budget.

Continuous Learning and Improvement

Emphasize continuous learning and improvement throughout the development process. Encourage the team to share lessons learned, identify areas for improvement, and explore new research or technologies that can enhance the capabilities of your NLP AI tool. Continuously monitor user feedback and iterate on the tool based on user needs and evolving requirements.

Continuous learning and improvement are essential for keeping the AI-powered novel writing system up-to-date, relevant, and effective. This section outlines the key steps and strategies to foster a culture of learning and ensure the system evolves with advancements in NLP and user needs.

Stay Abreast of NLP Research:

Encourage the development team to stay updated with the latest research and advancements in Natural Language Processing (NLP). Attend conferences, workshops, and webinars related to NLP and AI writing technologies.

Continuous Integration of New Models:

Regularly assess and integrate new and improved language models into the system. Leverage pre-trained models and fine-tuning techniques to enhance the system's performance.

User Feedback and Iteration:

Gather user feedback and reviews from real-world users of the AI writing system. Analyze feedback to identify areas for improvement and prioritize feature enhancements based on user needs.

A/B Testing and Experimentation:

Implement A/B testing to compare the performance of different algorithms, models, or features. This approach helps validate changes and improvements before full integration.

Address Bias and Ethical Concerns:

Continuously monitor the system for potential biases and ethical concerns in generated content. Implement techniques to minimize bias and ensure content aligns with ethical guidelines.

Collaborate with NLP Experts:

Collaborate with NLP researchers and experts to gain insights into cutting-edge techniques and methodologies. Engage in discussions and knowledge sharing to improve system capabilities.

Bug Tracking and Issue Resolution:

Maintain a robust bug tracking system to capture and address issues promptly. Implement a version control system to manage code changes and track bug fixes.

Data Quality Control:

Regularly review and update the dataset used for training and fine-tuning. Ensure data quality and relevance to avoid degradation in system performance.

System Performance Monitoring:

Set up monitoring tools to track system performance, response times, and resource utilization. Use these metrics to identify bottlenecks and areas for optimization.

Continuous Deployment:

Utilize Continuous Integration/Continuous Deployment (CI/CD) pipelines to facilitate regular and automated deployment of updates and improvements to the system.

Maintain User Guides and Documentation:

Keep user guides and documentation up-to-date with new features and improvements. Ensure that users have access to the latest information on system functionalities.

Training and Skill Development:

Encourage team members to participate in relevant training programs to enhance their skills in NLP, AI, and software development. Support continuous learning and growth.

Evaluate Business Impact:

Regularly evaluate the business impact of the AI writing system. Assess its contribution to productivity, user satisfaction, and overall organizational goals.

By implementing a continuous learning and improvement strategy, the AI-powered novel writing system can adapt to changing user needs, emerging technologies, and advancements in NLP, ensuring that it remains a valuable and effective tool for writers and content creators.

Collaborating with a team of experts or hiring professionals with the necessary skills can accelerate the development process and increase the chances of building a successful NLP AI tool for novel writing. Leveraging the collective expertise, diverse perspectives, and shared knowledge can lead to innovative solutions and enhance the overall quality of your tool.

Milton Keynes UK
Ingram Content Group UK Ltd.
UKHW020807150823
426904UK00017B/819